Terry Venables

FRED VENABLES

TERRY VENABLES:

Son of Fred

WEIDENFELD AND NICOLSON · LONDON

First published in Great Britain in 1990 by
George Weidenfeld & Nicolson Ltd,
91 Clapham High Street, London SW4 7TA

British Library Cataloguing in Publication Data
is available on request

ISBN 0 297 81159 2

Printed and bound in Great Britain by
Butler & Tanner Ltd, Frome and London

Contents

Illustrations

1

*P*eople often ask me if I am proud of my son Terry, and
my answer is always the same. I would have been proud of
Terry if his achievements in sport and in life had stopped
with winning the egg and spoon race at his primary school.
He could have followed me into a job in the docks or driving
a lorry and it would have made no difference. But I'll admit
there have been many times in the past twenty years when it
has been hard not to stand up in a crowd and shout: 'That's
my boy!'

I would count the night Terry won the title as manager of
Barcelona as one of the greatest times of my life, and my only
regret is that I wasn't there to share it with him. I was on
holiday in Wales, biting my nails, and nervous as hell for
Terry. I have never claimed to be a football expert but even
I could see what a feat it would be if he, an Englishman, could
lift the Spanish Championship in his first year as manager. We

had TV cameras set up in my pub, The Royal Oak in Chingford, and more cameras trailing me about on my holidays. It must have been just gone nine o'clock when the call came, not from Terry, but from a friend of ours, Tony, whose aunt was my manageress at the pub – Barcelona had done it! Within minutes I was on the phone to him, and that weekend travelled out there myself.

The city was alive. They even photographed me as I arrived at the airport. 'Papa Venables' the headline read. It was astonishing because my picture made the front page of Barcelona's leading sports paper and you had to turn three pages in to find news of Sevvy Ballesteros, a Spaniard, and the world's greatest golfer, who had just won a tournament.

When the Barcelona team arrived home over one million people were estimated to have lined their route from the airport to the town square and the journey took five hours to complete. That night, I admit, I did go to bed the proudest father in the world, bursting with it in a way I can hardly explain. Put it like this: eleven boys go out to play for England, watched by eleven beaming fathers in the stand; but there's only one manager of Barcelona, and that night there was only one Terry Venables. It had taken more than twenty years of total dedication and hard work, but winning the Spanish title with Barcelona made it worthwhile. I tell you this – it beat the hell out of the egg and spoon race!

The Spanish League Championship trophy may have been the most glamorous pot Terry has yet got his hands on, but I can still remember the first cup and medal he won as a footballer – and it was much bigger. He would have been twelve when he captained Dagenham Boys to win the Clark Cup, a huge great thing which for some reason finished up under my bed for safe-keeping. By then I knew how interested he had become in football. Everywhere he went he carried a little tennis ball, and he'd kick it as he ran along the street. We lived at 170 Bonham Road in Dagenham, and when I sent him round the corner to the shop to get me a packet of cigarettes, out would come the ball. Off he'd run, dribbling it down the street, so intent on this tennis ball he would scarcely look where he was going. One day I remember he ran straight into a post office box, catching his face on the lip and opening a huge wound. We had to take him to hospital to get it stitched up, but he could just as easily have run under a bus for all the attention he paid to his surroundings when he had that ball at his feet.

We were a very happy family. I was in the Navy when Terry was born on 6 January 1943 at 313 Vallance Avenue, Dagenham – my mother-in-law's house. It was during the war and I had been drafted into the special service from working on the Merchant Cruisers. I was in Nova Scotia, Canada, when the news came through that Terry, my first and only child, had arrived. It was a while before I could get out of the Navy. We were patrolling down to Bermuda with the US tenth task force. But I'm sure no father needs to be told of the delight I felt when I first set eyes on my son. It was very difficult for us all with me in the Navy, a new baby and little money coming into the household. My in-laws, Millie and Ossie, were very supportive and Terry's mum worked hard in a café to make sure we had enough to live on. But looking back I wonder how we pulled through.

I recall sitting in our tiny council house breaking up old dog-ends from the ashtray because I couldn't afford proper smokes of my own. My ship was based in Chatham, Kent, for some time and even the two-shilling fare was a struggle to find. But Myrtle was a good housekeeper, always making sure she had a bit put by so I could afford the return journey. Like most families during the war it was a case of making do and no-one complained because you knew there were others in the same boat – and some even worse off.

I left the Navy at the end of the war and got a job driving lorries for a weekly wage of six pounds. It sounds a pittance now, not even the price of a round of drinks, but at the time it was more money than I had earned in my life. I'd done everything until then, made washers for tuppence an hour, worked as a van boy, even delivered papers door to door in the evening. I was a junior porter on a station, sweeping up after people mostly, rode a bike and delivered groceries for Sainsbury's in Ilford. Earning six pounds a week as a lorry driver I thought I was well off, although I had to walk to work every day because I couldn't afford the bus fare. I made up for lost time with Terry by taking him out with me whenever I could, even though he was very small. A friend of mine, Tom Griffiths, had an old tipper truck and he used to travel round the area buying up scrap. Any spare time I had I would borrow the truck and take Terry out for rides. I'd hoist him up in the back and we'd drive around together. He loved it. I suppose big trucks are glamorous to kids. Terry would even get a kick out of sweeping it out – he used to ask to do it. So old Tom got his van cleaned up for nothing as well.

I think the first time I saw Terry kick a ball was at the age of three, but it would be lying to say I knew then he had the talent. I've got to admit it was his granddad Ossie who really nurtured his interest in the game. His mum still worked in the café and I was on the lorries. Myrtle's parents would look after him all day. The old man used to take him out to the park, and I suppose it was there he first found the inspiration that would make him become a professional footballer.

Ossie had been a tremendous athlete in his younger days. He was from Wales, mid-Rhondda, and it always came as a surprise to me that he was a big football man, not rugby as you would expect. He was a runner too and a fine one in his prime. I'd say it was Ossie who encouraged Terry to take his sport seriously. He'd go over the park for a game of football, sometimes even take him to his club for a frame or two of snooker, and when Terry came home to us at the end of the day he was full of it. We were all interested, of course, but never dreamt of where this new-found passion might lead. It seemed strange to me at first, because it was only a few years earlier that he had shown no interest at all in football when I took him to watch Barking Town play. I had played in goal for Barking and was always more keen on the amateur game than watching the professionals play up the road at West Ham or Tottenham.

This one day I took Terry to Barking – his first football match – thinking he would love every second. I couldn't have been more wrong! I don't think he had watched the game for more than a minute or two before showing his total lack of interest by clambering all over the seats around us. Thinking about it he hasn't changed much in all these years – always more of a doer than a watcher. Sitting in the stand at Barking bored him, but, once he got a pair of football boots on and began to play himself, we hardly saw him from one day to the next. He started the way all young boys start, turning out for his school, Lymington. Ossie remained a faithful fan and I remember spending afternoons standing in the mud and the rain watching Terry play half-back. We'd drag the nets out and put the goalposts up before kick-off, then hang around to take them all down again once the final whistle went – it was a lot less strenuous watching Barking, I can tell you.

Terry would have been eleven when he played his début game for Lymington and it was there I first met his school-master George Jackson – a man who had a great influence on Terry in his young life. Jackson coached Lymington's football team and the way he acted you would have thought he was managing Manchester United. He was an ex-pilot who had lost a leg in the war when he was twenty-two and he'd stand on the touchline, with the walking stick he used as a crutch, getting absolutely furious if the boys did anything wrong. He was a fanatical Spurs supporter and a strict disciplinarian. Terry used to joke that you daren't cross him or take the mickey out of him otherwise you'd end up with a wooden leg yourself!

Terry was his star pupil, and Jackson would get very angry, hollering and shouting, if he thought Terry wasn't pulling his weight. I'd be standing right next to him as he waved his stick at Terry and shouted instructions. But I never said anything – he was usually right! But it made the strangest sight, Jackson hobbling up and down the touchline in a rage screaming his head off at these eleven-year-old kids. One day he got so irate he smashed the stick into the ground in a fury and it snapped completely in two! Good old George, he was a nice guy really and Terry still gets letters from him. We've got a lot to thank him for despite his cantankerous behaviour, because it was George's influence that pushed Terry into the Dagenham Schools team and really got his career started.

By this time the football bug had bitten him completely, and it was as much as we could do to keep up with all his dirty laundry. Ossie and I would fetch his boots home and clean them meticulously after every match while his mum would wash his gear. Football was the most important thing in his life and his mum and I saved as much as we could to make sure he always had the right kit and the best boots. I was working at weekends driving to Manchester and back in this rickety old lorry. I'd leave at five o'clock Saturday morning and get back in the early hours of Sunday, but it was all money and it did help. We'd scrounge the cash for Terry's stuff if we had to but we always made sure we paid it back. We never owed anybody a penny and that's something I've stuck to even to this day.

It wasn't just football – Terry played cricket as well and

competed in long-distance running – it made him a right Jack-the-lad at Lymington and I suppose his schoolwork suffered because of it. Not that he was ever a bad boy, but he'd get in regular trouble with the headmaster for looking out of the window or rushing through his work so he could get out on the sports field again. The only other subject he showed real interest in was woodwork, in fact I've still got a little table he made for me at Lymington. Whenever he sees it he tells me the same thing: 'Look at that dad,' he'll say, 'tongued and grooved.' He even made a new leg for sports-master George!

As captain of Lymington School, and under the influence of George Jackson, Terry was a natural for the Dagenham district line-up, and the year he made the grade they played East Ham for the Clark Cup. That's got to be one of the grandest trophies I've seen in my life – the boys could hardly carry it once it was won. We all stood there looking at this massive piece of silverware and no-one quite knew what to do with it, no-one wanted to take responsibility in case it got lost, and that was how it ended up under my bed for most of the season. That was the first real trophy Terry won as a footballer and even then I refused to believe there could be many more. He must have been thirteen when I first realized we could have a star of the future on our hands. The Dagenham Schools connection got him an invite to train with West Ham twice a week and he would make the trip after school with a couple of his team-mates. We knew it was only a small beginning, but even my untrained eye was recognizing that Terry was turning into a special sort of player.

For a start, he was playing regular park kickabout matches with local lads a lot older than him – and what talent we had in Dagenham at that time! You could have picked an all-star team from the lads living a few roads near us, and many of the short-trousered boys who knocked on my door to ask if

Terry wanted a game, went on to become household names themselves.

Ken Brown, who played for West Ham and later successfully managed Norwich City, lived only five doors away from us in Bonham Road. Bill Allen lived in the house opposite and his sons Les and Dennis went on to play for Tottenham and Reading respectively. Now they are middle-aged men with sons of their own – Clive at Manchester City and Martin at West Ham. The Coney's lived down our road, too, the old man playing for Fulham, and now young Dean who has had a good career with Fulham, Queens Park Rangers and Norwich. Martin Peters's dad, Bill, lived just down the block from us, and Jimmy Greaves's family were also from our area; although they moved to Hainault when he was quite young. People talk about the north-east as the hotbed of soccer, but in those days little Dagenham took some beating – a future England manager, Sir Alf Ramsey, came from our patch, and Dick Walker, then Tottenham's scout, was a local man.

But it was the Allen boys and Ken Brown, amongst others, who would most often come knocking for Terry, then they'd all go up the road to Vallance Park or Castle Green for a game. There were always kids over there, hanging around looking for a match, and it would often go on until it was too dark to see the ball. They were the keenest bunch of boys you ever saw, most of them older than Terry, but he was a big lad and he gave as good as he got.

The only serious injury he ever suffered then, was one summer when he got a kick in the face and came home in such a state we could hardly recognize him. His face resembled a mask, with two little slits for his eyes, a third for his mouth and two tiny holes where his nose used to be. It was a terrifying sight, and we were desperately worried for him. As we took him up the hospital, his mum turned to me and said:

'He won't want to play football again after this lot.' But as soon as the doctor had bandaged him up his first question was: 'Can I go over the park now, mum?' Stopping him joining the games with the Browns and Allens was the worst punishment we could give Terry in those days.

If his mum was really annoyed with him, she'd shut him upstairs in the bedroom and tell the other boys he couldn't come out. It must have been torture for him. He couldn't see those games from his room, but he could hear them – the racket they made echoed around Dagenham – and it must have driven him mad knowing he couldn't be part of it. Being bored he would get up to all sorts of tricks up there, climbing out of the tiny window, along a ledge, and in through another – until he was reported by a next-door neighbour and told off by his mum again. The neighbour was known as Bertie Smalls – after the supergrass! – and the very next week Terry was in trouble with her again. One of his little games was to launch a catapult from our back to our own front garden and a misfired missile went through her window. She refused to believe it wasn't done on purpose!

He was still training with West Ham then and, although I'd let him go to watch their youth team play, I still felt he was too small at thirteeen to watch the first-team matches. It meant he couldn't see his heroes, the stars of the day, so he made up for it by travelling to the main London railway stations to get their autographs as they came off the train. He knew exactly what teams came to what stations: Manchester United to Euston, Newcastle United to King's Cross; and when and where all the big London clubs would be returning from their away matches. He had every player's signature, and four or five years later, when he was on the verge of breaking into Chelsea's first team under Ted Drake, he still had that book. His progress was so rapid that he probably played against many of the men whose autographs he collected just a few years before.

Not that Terry was ever surprised at how quickly things happened for him. I'd say he knew even then he was going to be a professional footballer – it was all he talked about. I remember one teacher at school, Mr Warren, asking him to write an essay on what he wanted to be when he grew up. The rest of the class wrote pages, Terry a single line: 'When I grow up I am going to become a footballer.' Mr Warren saw his effort, tut-tutted a few times and told him: 'I've seen thousands of essays like this, from thousands of boys like you, Terry ... one in a million become footballers.' Terry looked him straight in the eye, 'I'm that one in a million,' he replied, 'someone's got to be a footballer, why shouldn't it be me?' More tut-tuts from Mr Warren, 'Please yourself,' he said, 'but you'll learn.' I wonder how that schoolteacher felt the day Terry stepped out on to the field as captain of Chelsea, or the day he made his first appearance for England – probably like the record producer who told The Beatles they'd never make it!

Terry was sure of his future; as far as he was concerned he was already playing with what could be termed the 'big boys'. He often played over the park with eighteen- or nineteen-year-old chaps, men who had been working four or five years while he was still at school. They had a goalkeeper known as Big Charlie who Terry remembers as the most relaxed man he's ever seen on a football field. This team were hot stuff and Charlie was never used. He'd lean on a goalpost watching the action on the other pitches, or sometimes he'd read a book. On one occasion when the team won 19–0, Big Charlie even had time to leave his goal and wander over to another game to have a chat with one of his mates. Terry scored twice in that match and I think it made his day to get on the scoresheet in a game with the older boys.

Even then, you could see the manager in Terry coming out. The other boys over the parks would be a lot older, yet you'd still hear Terry getting them organized. He'd tell the players where to play and what to do; everyone looked up to him. Our house became the regular meeting-place for all the football-mad boys in the area, and Terry always had a tennis ball in his pocket just in case anyone fancied a game.

It was then that we started to get all the scouts coming round to speak to Terry personally. West Ham had been keeping a close watch on him, but his performances for Dagenham Boys created pandemonium in our household. It was then that I first met the man who would eventually take him to Chelsea – Jimmy Thompson.

2

Jim was a magnificent character, a former Chelsea centre-forward himself, who had the reputation as the finest talent-spotter of the day. He had discovered players like Jimmy Greaves, Les Allen, Peter Brabrook, and Tony Nicholas and made successes of them all; and he sized-up Terry straight away. Had it not been for Jimmy Thompson I'm sure Terry would have finished up at West Ham. Terry knew the club and the staff there had always been very good to Myrtle and me. Their chairman, Reg Pratt, often invited us to watch games as his guest and at one match Myrtle sat in the directors' box next to Dame Anna Neagle. Oh yes, West Ham were as friendly as they come – but Jimmy was Chelsea's secret weapon. He was such a character and so different from the others, you couldn't help but like him.

Most of the top clubs sent talent scouts to watch Dagenham Boys play because they had such a strong side and they'd all stand on the touchline discussing the game. There would be Dick Walker, a regular from Arsenal, and people from as far afield as Manchester United and Wolves. You could spot the scouts a mile off comparing notes, talking about the games they'd seen that week, and passing judgement on different players – but not Jim. I'd arrive in my beaten-up old van – no insurance, no tax disc on the windscreen – and I'd hear a whispering coming from the long grass behind the goal as I walked past. 'Fred, Fred, come here, get down quick. Don't let anyone see you, don't let them know I'm here.' It would be Jim, lying on his stomach, surreptitiously eyeing the talent. Once I was down there he'd become more relaxed; 'Hello Mr Venables, how are you? Terry's playing well.' That was typical Jim, always ducking and diving. I've never met a man so much on the move. But I still don't know what he was so secretive about because you couldn't miss Jim. He lived in Gidea Park and never owned a car, he'd walk everywhere bedecked in bowler hat, smart coat, striped trousers and carrying an umbrella – you could hardly call that travelling incognito.

His expertise didn't end with football, Jim could also tell you what horses to back if you were a racing man. He was a professional punter for the lords and ladies of the day and he used to go to all the big meetings. I don't know if Jim was a heavy gambling man himself but he'd devised a scheme at the races where he couldn't lose. If a big punter wanted £1,000 placed on a horse, Jim would take the chit and place it with the bookie. If the horse won he collected his commission out of the punter's winnings, if it lost he'd get a cut off the bookie for using his services – it was a foolproof scheme to make money.

That was the sort of man he was. He could look at a footballer and tell you his form, look at a racehorse and do the same. I suppose his need for secrecy came because he knew the rest of football were watching his every move, waiting to see who he would go after next. I can remember one day when he arranged to meet Terry at a hotel and take him for lunch; a simple exercise you would think, but not for Jim. Terry was waiting in the lobby when he heard this voice behind him talking at ninety miles an hour. Jim, of course, in full swing, saying: 'Come on Terry, follow me son, over here, through here, turn right, now left...' and there was Terry running through the corridors of this hotel, through swing doors and out fire exits to keep up until Jim could be certain that no-one was following them.

He would have us in fits of laughter sometimes with his antics. In those days the scouts would often call round to our little mid-terrace council place in Bonham Road, have a cup of tea and chat with Terry just to keep their name and their club fresh in our minds. Jim was the same but he hated anyone knowing he was there. There would be a knock on the door and Jim would jump up from his chair, hissing 'I'm not here, I'm not here. I'll go and hide in the bathroom until they're gone.' 'It's all right Jim,' I would tell him, 'so what if you're in our house, what difference does it make?' But he would never have it: 'No, I'll stay in the bathroom, Fred,' he'd insist, 'I don't want them to know I'm here.' Then he would disappear for ages, cooped up in our titchy bathroom until the other scout had gone.

Jim was a marvellous man in many ways, but I'll also never forget him as the man who almost ended Terry's career before it began. He came round to our house one night to find Terry with a very swollen sore foot in a bucket of ice. He had broken a bone (not that we knew at the time) but all Jim could see was that he would miss his next game of football. 'That's no good,' he told us when he saw the state Terry was in, 'he's got an important match coming up.' So Jim began massaging the foot and he worked on it for ages. 'That should work now,' he said, 'that'll fetch the bruise out.' Then he took Terry out into the back garden. 'Kick that ball,' he ordered, 'run and kick it as hard as you can.' You could tell by Terry's face he was none too sure about this, but Jim was the boss so he did what he was told. Jim was insisting he'd get him fit for a match in three nights time. Terry was looking suspiciously at him and in the end you could see from Terry's expression what he was thinking: 'To hell with it, he knows what he's doing.' He ran up and gave this ball a clout. All I can remember is the minute his boot made contact with the leather he went cross-eyed in agony and nearly passed out! He has later told me he'd never experienced so much pain before or since. But I can't say Jim was lying when he promised to fetch the bruise out, because Terry's foot went so black after that we thought it was going to drop off. He probably broke another three bones with that one kick! Anyway, his mum insisted we take him to the hospital for an X-ray, where we received the proper diagnosis of a broken bone.

However, that still didn't stop Jim. He kept coming round the house with this stuff he had got from the chemist. I don't know how he got his hands on it because it was strong enough to be only available on prescription ... but that was Jim. Anyway, working on the basis of being once bitten and twice shy, Terry let the foot heal in its own time. Jim was some chief scout, but he was no physio!

That doctor must have done a good job, though, because two weeks later Terry was up and about and playing in the London schoolboys' trials, his first step on the road to many appearances for England at that level. Jim was still in the background telling Terry not to talk to this scout or that scout and trying to put him off signing for Manchester United or Tottenham because the interest in Terry throughout the country was just incredible.

The papers were calling it the hottest hunt for a young star since Stanley Matthews signed for Stoke almost 30 years earlier. Terry had hardly reached his fifteenth birthday and there wasn't a club in England that hadn't heard of him. Not just the scouts were coming now, but managers and chairmen of some of the biggest sides in Britain: Stan Cullis, Jimmy Murphy, Bill Nicholson, Ted Drake, Arthur Rowe, and Peter Doherty could be seen at our games, all with their sights focused on signing Terry. When he was playing in London I got to his matches whenever I could, often leaving work for a couple of hours and returning as soon as the final whistle had gone. Ossie would get on a train or bus and go as far as Luton if it meant seeing his precious grandson in action.

It wasn't long before transport became the last of our worries – clubs were happy to pay for us to see Terry's games as their guests. We went to Ireland with Manchester United, and Chelsea took us to Preston to see an England schoolboys game; in those days it was the only way we could afford to go. There were other offers and financial inducements made to me and Terry's mum if we could persuade him to sign for a particular club. Scouts would hide around the corner from our house and as soon as we came through the door they'd be in after us promising to do this or that for Terry. The spiel would always be the same – they'd promise us money or a car if Terry signed for them, but we never found their offers tempting.

We always knew that Terry would make up his own mind and sign for the club he chose. Sure he'd talk it over with Myrtle and me, and the three of us often discussed his options as a footballer, but Terry would have the final say. What's the point of driving around in a nice new car if your son is stuck at a club going nowhere? I'd never be able to live with myself if I had put Terry's career in jeopardy for a bit of money of my own. But that didn't stop the rumours and innuendo. People would hint at what other boys' parents had been given or what the boy himself had received. They seemed to think that we were out to cop the same. I got sick of explaining a new car didn't mean anything to us, or to Terry, and when he finally signed for Chelsea, at the age of seventeen, he did so for the most boyish of reasons – a lot of his mates went there.

However, that was in the future. At fifteen Terry was training with as many different clubs as he could, including Chelsea, West Ham, Spurs, Fulham, and Arsenal, and ploughing all his efforts into making that England Schoolboys side.

He was dedicated in a way that separated him from many of his contemporaries. For a start he only drank orangeade, never alcohol. He had been in local working men's clubs and pubs with us from a very early age, but even as a young man he was still a teetotaller. Some of his mates would take the mickey and try to get him to have a beer, but he never touched the stuff. Nor did we have any worries about him smoking. That had always been a vice of mine, but I made sure that if Terry was going to take up a career as a professional footballer he would never be tempted to follow me down the same path.

When I heard that some of his mates at school had started smoking I took immediate action. We were sitting in the house in Bonham Road one night when I tried out my plan. 'Do you want a cigarette, Terry?' I asked, 'have one of mine.' 'No thanks dad,' he said, but I was insistent. 'Go on ... have a puff,' I told him. As soon as the smoke hit his lungs he turned green and I thought he was going to be physically sick. 'Right,' I said, 'now don't let me ever catch you in any of those shop doorways having a fag with the other lads.' It worked. Not that you had to work too hard on Terry as a rule, in those days he would have been any manager's dream, making sacrifices few boys his age would even consider.

One week we bought him a new bike called a New Yorker,

it was bright red and really smart. He rode on it every day to the park for his games of football and then off to the chippy to buy fish and chips and a bottle of Tizer for his supper, or sometimes pie and mash. He absolutely cherished that bike until one day when Jimmy Thompson paid us a visit. As soon as he set eyes on the New Yorker his face dropped. 'Whose is that?' he asked. When told it was Terry's Jimmy retorted 'You shouldn't ride a bike, it's bad for your muscles. Your hamstrings will tighten up.' Terry put the brand new red bike away, and never so much as put a foot on it after that.

Even when he got older he remained the same and always kept a clear sense of what was good for him as an athlete and what wasn't. The regular feature of Friday nights was a card game at my house with Terry and all his mates. Terry would never go out to the pub but he'd stay up with us playing cards and then go to bed at ten o'clock on the dot. Every Friday was the same, he always got in bed early because of his match the next day while the other lads stayed on to finish the game. A lot of them played football as well, but they were never as dedicated as Terry. It was funny, for as soon as Terry went to bed they used to gang up on me to try to win because they knew it would get me wild. Terry's mates knew all the tricks and they'd wind me up rotten, he must have heard the noise and the shouting and laughing from his bedroom upstairs but it never persuaded him to come down. Saturday was matchday and he needed his sleep.

Even today Terry has kept in touch with a lot of those boys. Ronnie Handley, who went to Chelsea with him but wasn't good enough to turn pro, finished up as Basildon Town's longest serving manager. I got him a job on the docks when his pro career ended and he's still working there. But of an evening he'd always be out training players or scouting for Basildon – he was their answer to Matt Busby!

There was another boy opposite called Joe Jennings whose father was a street bookmaker. The old man used to take small bets – thruppence each way – on street corners (which was illegal) and you'd always see him dashing in and out of buildings when the police were after him. Young Joe, Peter Auger and Billy Adkins used to come knocking for Terry, and Joe had the worst singing voice in the world. Terry told us that in school assembly the teachers used to make Joe mime to the hymns, because his singing would upset the rest of the kids. Terry had a mischievous sense of humour and when Joe came round he'd say: 'Make him sing mum, go on ask Joe to sing.' When Joe opened his mouth this terrible wailing sound would come out and Myrtle would give him a bit of cake for his efforts, or maybe just to shut him up! When Joe left school he went off to Epsom to become a jockey and a lot of the local lads would go down to the track to see him. They had some good times together but Joe's career as a jockey didn't work out and finally he followed his dad into the bookmaking business. But he made a better job of it than the old man ever had and now he's a huge success with a chain of bookies' shops.

A lot of the local lads have made successes of themselves but the star attraction at the time was Terry. His performance for London had got him picked for the England schoolboys' trials in Doncaster. It came at a time when he was just ready to leave school and before he left a teacher from Lymington contacted Myrtle. 'I need to talk to you, Mrs Venables,' she said, 'all your boy does is look out of the window and all he thinks about is football. We think he's good enough to stay on at school but we need to know what his intentions are now. Is he going to concentrate on his schoolwork, or is he just going to waste his time playing football?' Myrtle stood firm: 'He has trials for England schoolboys this week,' she said, 'one in a thousand boys get the chance of that. If he doesn't make it he'll stay on at school. But we've got to give him that chance.'

The three of us travelled up to Doncaster that day and the further away from London we got the harder the snow came down – talk about the frozen north! We stayed at a little hotel near the ground which seemed to be slap-bang in the middle of Doncaster racetrack. A representative from one of the top London football clubs came with us just to make sure the facilities were all right and we didn't want for anything. In those days we carried about a tiny pair of Terry's boots we'd bought for him when he was ten. They were our lucky mascot, and they came with us throughout his youthful career. Many years later they even made an appearance on Grandstand when Terry reached the FA Cup Final as manager of Queens Park Rangers! I've still got them in a cupboard upstairs in the pub and whenever I get them out they remind me of that freezing cold day in Doncaster.

When we turned up at the ground I had a look around the main stand: the number of scouts and managers present far outnumbered the fans. It was probably the strongest indication I had yet of how far Terry was down the road to becoming a professional footballer. I didn't know if Terry was nervous or not, you ask a kid how he's feeling and he tells you 'I'm all right, dad.' Who is to know what is really going on inside? But I can remember he didn't play as if he was nervous and they picked him six times for England schoolboys that year.

A lot of people were talking of Terry as the next Duncan Edwards. He was a big lad for fifteen, weighing eleven-and-a-half stone and standing five feet and nine inches. He had a powerful shot on him – fierce even at that level. As a very small kid he had broken a staff room window at his junior school playing football with a tennis ball and it had travelled at such a lick the teachers refused to believe he had not thrown it on purpose. As he got older his shot gained in strength and the coaches at the Football Association made him vice-captain of the team almost immediately. We had some great times watching him in action for the schoolboys team that year although I'll admit I always seemed to be more nervous than Terry.

One of the proudest days of my life was seeing his first game for the schoolboys at Wembley against a Scotland team that included Billy Bremner. Sitting in the royal box at Wembley the goals looked so big and the pitch so wide for such little boys. A lump came to my throat as they walked out and I was very, very worried for Terry. There was an odd mixture of onlookers in the box – ancient FA councillors (some of whom are still about!) sitting next to anxious looking mums and dads, and the scouts taking notes as the game proceeded. You could spot the parents a mile off. Before the kick-off they all looked like expectant fathers in the waiting-room off a maternity ward. Everyone was pacing up and down, smoking too many cigarettes and saying 'Oh my God, I hope he plays well today.' Even Terry looked small on that pitch and there was always the fear that so much hard work could come to nothing for the sake of one bad match. All those times he had come home with big black toe nails from kicking a ball too heavy for him, the broken foot, the cuts, the stitches in his face, and trainers who didn't know a thing about football injuries and thought the cure-all treatment for every knock was to plonk the boy's foot in a bucket of iced water and let him get on with it. Those were the thoughts that went through my mind as I watched my son play at Wembley and there wasn't a damn thing I could do to help him.

He was outstanding, and at the end of the game I couldn't speak I was so proud of my little boy. It was a different world for me. After the game, the FA officials and the scouts got the brandy out for the mums and dads but, although I needed it, I never touched a drop. I could hardly afford a pint of beer in those days and I felt even guiltier touching their brandy. Terry was with me saying: 'What do you think of that dad, good isn't it?' He seemed so calm compared to me.

However, it was coming to the time for that big decision: which of the many interested clubs would Terry choose to sign for? West Ham were his local side and he enjoyed his training sessions there under the man who would one day give him his first job in soccer management – Malcolm Allison. Arsenal were among the first to approach us and Terry had trained regularly with them at London Colney and Southgate. Tottenham were the club he supported as a boy, his schoolmaster George Jackson was a fan and the inspirational Dave Mackay was his hero. Chelsea had many of his mates on their staff and good old Jimmy Thompson blowing in his ear every two minutes. Or would it be Manchester United? What kid could fail to be impressed by a place like Old Trafford or a manager like Sir Matt Busby? A lot of nice things have been written about Sir Matt and I can vouch for all of them. Throughout our dealings with United he was never anything less than the perfect gentleman and never put Terry under any pressure to sign.

Early on in Terry's England schoolboy career United paid for me and Myrtle to fly all the way to Windsor Park in Belfast to watch him play. They took us to Manchester by train and then flew us to Belfast to watch the match. I can remember being met at the hotel by United's big Northern Ireland international goalkeeper Harry Gregg whose duty it was to look after us during the trip. Harry had a big family and there were loads of his kids running riot around this hotel. But United never gave us the hard sell; they just took us to the match and got us back home again safely. I think Sir Matt realized we were ordinary people and this was the only way we had of watching our son play. I met him not so long ago at a Football Association function and as so many years had passed I didn't think he would remember me. But he came straight up, shook my hand and asked if I remembered him! I got his autograph that night, and Bobby Charlton's, they are marvellous men and I have always thought of United as a great club.

Some people say it's better to go to a small club and learn your trade in a more intimate atmosphere rather than get thrown in at the deep end with one of the bigger sides. I always felt Terry made the right choice with Chelsea. Many of his friends, including Allan Harris, who would later become his assistant at Queens Park Rangers, Barcelona, and Spurs, went there and the youth team system built by Dick Foss had many of the stars of the day. In the end it was a straight choice between Chelsea and West Ham and Terry made up his mind in typically defiant style.

'All my mates are going to Chelsea, dad,' he told me in our front room at Bonham Road. 'It's a good club. I know the people and I'll like it there. That's where I'm going!'

So we got in touch with their manager Ted Drake and Terry signed the next day with our blessing.

3

*A*s soon as it was announced that Terry had signed for Chelsea we had many of the other clubs on the phone or on the knocker trying to get the deal nullified. The stakes had been getting higher and higher in the weeks leading up to the decision but now they were really going mad. I could understand their reasoning because Terry had obviously become the jewel in the England schoolboys crown. But what annoyed me most were the snide comments of some of the other boys' fathers who thought we had all been paid to take Terry to Chelsea. I suppose at that stage everyone thinks their son is a Jimmy Greaves but I wasn't quite ready for some of the back-stabbing that went on. People would rudely say to you: 'How come Terry got to Chelsea and my son didn't?' and you had to be strong-willed not to lose your temper with them.

I was a foreman with a meat company on the docks and

therefore easy to seek out. People wanted to row with me about Chelsea and about football all the time and it was then I realized that life couldn't help but change in some way if your son became a professional footballer. Of course, there was a good side. I'd come home from work in my little old van and there would be neighbours and friends asking after Terry, saying they read reports in the papers of how well he was doing, making predictions about a rosy future. One phrase came up time and time again: 'You must be ever so proud of him.'

Not that the attention made much difference to Terry. For a start, he had only signed amateur forms with Chelsea. It was his ambition to make the England football team at the 1960 Olympics and to do that he knew he couldn't join up as a professional. Of course it meant he didn't have the money a lot of the other boys were on, so he had to take part-time jobs to supplement his income. He spent two summers as the attendant at the swimming pool in Barking park. I used to drop him off at half-past seven from my van on the way to work and he'd be over there until the park shut, cleaning the pool and making sure all the cubicles were spotless. Then, when he was finished, he'd come home and the pair of us would go out together training. I'd ride his bike – remember the bright red New Yorker? – and he would run alongside me from Bonham Road to the bus garage at Barking, down into Vallance Avenue and back to our house. We used to practise what footballers call 'doggies'. I would shout 'go' and he would sprint for a hundred yards; 'stop' and he would jog, then it would be 'go' again and so on. He would do that three or four nights a week as well as holding down his job at the pool.

During the winter his time was completely taken up with football. He'd travel up to London by train with a lot of friends from Dagenham who had office jobs in the city. They even devised little schemes to help him improve his fitness. As Terry came to his stop the other lads would hold him back until the doors were about to close, then they'd let him go and he'd have to run like a maniac to get on to the platform in time! As Terry got faster so they would hold him for longer until he was sprinting like a greyhound.

All the while his career was progressing. He moved up from England schoolboys and began playing for the youth team, and he did go on to make one appearance for his country at amateur level in a match played at the famous non-League ground, Dulwich Hamlets in south London. In fact, Terry was still an amateur when he made his début for Chelsea at the age of sixteen-and-a-half. He had previously been playing for the youth and the B teams when one day he was told he was to get his chance in a game against West Ham. We all knew it would only be a matter of time before Terry started playing first-team football because the youth side had won everything possible, but I don't think anyone realized it would all happen so quickly.

Chelsea's manager Ted Drake, the old Arsenal player, was building a good young team along the lines of Manchester United's 'Busby Babes'. In Chelsea's case they were known as 'Drake's Ducklings' and they included some of the finest young players of the day, particularly Jimmy Greaves and Terry's Chelsea hero Johnny Brooks.

Actually Brooks features in a funny story that Terry told me about his début for Chelsea. Those who saw Brooks play would find it hard to believe that he suffered from a lack of confidence. He looked like Adonis, walked like John Wayne, and was probably the finest footballer in that Chelsea team. But Johnny was as nervous as hell and needed constant reassurance that he was having a good game. Anyway, Terry was sitting in the dressing-room at half-time during his first match for Chelsea – and he was very worried. Chelsea were winning 1–0 but he didn't think he was playing very well and was desperate for advice from one of the other players on what he should be doing. Terry cast his eyes around for assistance when suddenly he saw Johnny Brooks get up and begin this slow, loping film star's walk across to him. You can imagine the relief Terry felt. Of all people, his hero Johnny Brooks was going to come over and help him sort out his problem. He waited expectantly for these pearls of wisdom when Brooks arrived, sat down, put an arm around Terry and asked: 'How do you think I'm playing, Tel?' There and then, at sixteen-and-a-half, Terry tells me he realized you can forget talk about football being a team game; when it comes down to it, you're on your own!

Although that Chelsea side was young the manager Ted Drake was an experienced, wise man who acted as a father figure to his boys – and some of the parents too! Ted had a secretary, a man named John Battlesby, and it was like watching an English army general and his batman in action. They were both very smart men, very well-spoken and complete golf fanatics. Sometimes I'd go to see Ted in his huge long office at Stamford Bridge and he'd be there with John practising his swing. There was another office leading off from Ted's and they'd put a wastepaper basket on the desk and would chip plastic golf balls from one room to the other. Often you couldn't catch them at all in the afternoons because they'd be straight out and on to a golf course. If Terry ever had a problem, I wouldn't hesitate in going to Ted, he was a man you always felt you could get close to and wouldn't let you down. And Dick Foss did a magnificent job of looking after the young players with Jimmy Thompson.

By that time I was letting the professionals handle Terry's coaching – he was becoming a bit too dangerous for me. One day we went over Barking park, Terry had an England match coming up and wanted some extra practice. We put our coats down and I went in goal full of confidence with my memories of spectacular performances between the sticks for the local side. I was throwing myself this way and that when suddenly he caught one on the volley, and as I got a hand to it I felt this shooting pain go straight up my left arm. The force of the shot had pushed my hand back and strained the ligaments. I was off work for two weeks unable to lift a thing. That was when I brought a rather undignified end to my coaching career.

I suppose I was naïve in a lot of ways back then and I remember the day I found myself inadvertently making back-page news in the *Daily Express*. Terry had not been in the team long and he'd scored a goal in his last game against Cardiff City. I was working on the docks and there was a phone call for me. It was a reporter telling me that Drake had dropped Terry for the game on Saturday and asking what my thoughts were. My instant reaction was that it was news to me but he kept on with the questions: 'He scored a goal didn't he? Did you think he played well?' Finally he asked: 'Will you be speaking to Ted Drake about it?' 'Yes,' I said, 'I'll have a word with Ted.'

The next day it was all over the *Daily Express*: 'Angry Dad Slams Chelsea!' was the headline and I took plenty of stick over it at work. Everywhere I went people were calling out: 'There goes the Angry Dad, hello Angry Dad.' It upset me at first because the last person I was looking to cross was Ted Drake. He was such a placid man, such a fair man, who would always listen to other people's points of view. He was strict with the boys without being an ogre and always tried to bring them up in a way that would have pleased their mums and dads. Ted asked to see me after that and said: 'Fred, Terry has got some good points and some bad points. We'll iron those out in time, and once we think he's ready for it I'm sure he won't have a problem keeping his place.'

He was so good about it I wished I'd kept my mouth shut; and he was as good as his word.

Not that Ted took such a relaxed attitude about everything, far from it. Terry has told me a story about the Chelsea full-back of the day, Peter Sillett, being driven home by Drake. Ted was worried about something at the club and when the car stopped at a traffic light he sat there in silence for almost five minutes. Finally a policeman came over and asked Ted to wind down his window. 'What are you up to sir?' asked the copper, 'the lights have changed to green six times now.' 'My God, Peter,' said Ted, ashen-faced, 'I thought you were driving!'

It was Ted who established Terry as a regular in the Chelsea first-team and when the British Olympic side was picked without him, Terry went the whole hog and committed himself to the club as a professional. Earning wages of £18 in the summer and £20 during the season would hardly qualify you as a tax exile even in 1960, but Terry still had a lot of hangers-on trying to lure him into investing in businesses or to investigate dodgy-looking pension schemes.

That was the reasoning behind Terry registering himself as a limited company at the age of seventeen. It meant he handled his own future and he once said he couldn't under-stand why someone in a camel-hair overcoat should be able to take twenty per cent of his earnings. I'll admit his first few business ventures were a disaster. He bought some shares off a friend which failed, a tailor's shop died a death after about eighteen months, and his own idea – Thingamywigs – didn't last much longer. Terry and a partner had a plan to make a hat with a wig inside so that if a woman was wearing curlers she could leave the house without taking them out. The wigs were either blonde or dark brown and we all used to go around selling them. But the business couldn't last because once you had bought one you never needed to replace it. So that folded as well.

It was a different world for me, the former lorry driver from Dagenham. I would sit in the directors' box surrounded by rich and famous men like Joe Mears the chairman, and Richard Attenborough, watching Terry and Chelsea play. I was overawed by what went on but no-one ever made me feel unwelcome or uncomfortable and soon I began to enjoy it. Terry, too, was caught up in the glamour and at seventeen he won an award for young sports personalities and received an invitation to meet Prime Minister Harold Wilson at Downing Street.

I remember he jumped in a cab from Chelsea to take him to his audience with Britain's most powerful politician and when he gave the address the cabbie said sarcastically: 'I suppose you're going to number ten?' 'As a matter of fact, I am,' said Terry bold as brass. When the cab arrived he jumped out to be officially received at the home of the Prime Minister. Another time he was the star attraction at a fund-raising event for a new chest clinic held at the Room at the Top nightclub in Ilford. When we arrived the doorman refused Terry admission because he was too young!

Terry's happiest days at Chelsea were soon to end. Ted Drake left and in his place came Tommy Docherty – a man who couldn't have been more different. Ted might have been aloof sometimes but he was always consistent. You knew where you were with Ted. He phoned me at work to say he was leaving Chelsea. He said there was a problem and he had to leave. I was shocked ... after all those years he had served the club. When Terry came home he was very upset, he had a lot of feeling for Ted and now didn't know what to expect from the new man.

I don't think Terry has ever made much of a secret of the fact that he and Docherty didn't get on, but there was no reason to suspect this from our first meetings with him. Tom struck me as a man desperate to be liked. I remember travelling on the coach with him and his wife, and Docherty would be cracking jokes and keen to impress. He wanted to be seen as open and friendly, as one of the boys, something Ted always shied away from. I make Ted right because, looking back, Docherty brought most of his problems at Chelsea upon himself because of this approach.

One day he would want the boys to call him Tom, the next, boss, then the following day it would be back to Tom again. I don't call that discipline, I call it downright foolishness. I certainly felt he was jealous of Terry in particular. He seemed to resent Terry's influence on the rest of the team and his business interests outside of football. Tom thought he was a somebody as manager of Chelsea, and he seemed to resent anybody else who might get treated in the same way. Yet, at first, he seemed keen to have Terry on his side. He made him captain of the club, at just nineteen, a position that reflected the way many others at Chelsea looked up to him. Terry came home to Bonham Road delighted, telling us all how fantastic it was that he was skippering the side the next day. I can remember thinking this didn't sound at all like the Tommy Docherty others in football had told me about. I began to think they had got him wrong. But it was me who was making the mistake.

John Hollins, for instance, has told a story of Terry getting a rucking at full-time for changing Tom's tactics. He wanted the team playing a certain way, and it wasn't working. Terry changed the tactics on the field and Tom was furious. The fact that Chelsea won had nothing to do with it – Tom refused to tolerate anything that could be seen as undermining his authority. I noticed a change in Terry because of this incident.

When Ted Drake was in charge he would always listen to

what he had to say, whether or not he agreed with it. He'd mull it over in his mind, think about it, then come to a decision. But Terry and Docherty were so far apart that often he'd dismiss his thoughts out of hand. One minute Tom wanted to be your mate, the next he wanted to run the players into the ground with training and be the strict disciplinarian – Terry couldn't go for that change in personality. Terry would come home very upset about what was going on, he felt Docherty's way was unjust, and he also knew he had no way of talking it through with Tom. Drake was approachable, he would listen to your opinions, and give them respect even if he felt you were in the wrong, but Terry and Tom were too far apart for that gap to ever be bridged.

I would try to give Terry advice as best I could, because there was no way I could ever see him winning a war of words with the manager. I simply don't think he would ever get used to another boss after Ted. 'Docherty's the governor, now,' I would tell him. 'You've got to look at it from his point of view. Ted Drake's no longer about, and it's a fact of life that you'll have to get on with a new man. There's no mileage in saying you can't accept him or his methods – you've got to accept them both, because he now rules the roost at Stamford Bridge.' But Terry was Ted Drake's man through and through. Maybe it would have helped if Tom had involved Terry, as his captain, more in the tactical side of the game. Drake would discuss plans for set-pieces but Docherty ordered the team about as if they were children.

I suppose it is ironic that Terry also had some of his greatest successes under Docherty, as well as some of his biggest heartaches. It was in the Chelsea side of 1964, that he made his two appearances for the full England team against Belgium and Holland. Sir Alf Ramsey was the manager at the time, and he was another man that Terry didn't seem to get on with. I've always wondered if Terry's short full England career was partly my fault, for giving him a bit of duff advice about how to impress Ramsey. Knowing how poor his relationship was with Docherty, I was keen for Terry to get off on a good foot with his England boss.

Ramsey, too, was born and bred in Dagenham and I thought a little reminder of what the pair of them had in common wouldn't hurt. Before Terry left to join up with the England team I told him: 'Say to Ramsey that Sid sends his regards. He's a mate of mine, and he lived next door to Alf so he's bound to remember him. Tell him that and he's sure to take a shine to you.' So the first chance Terry had he sidled up to Ramsey and dropped it in. 'Oh, by the way, I was speaking to Sid your old next door neighbour in Dagenham, and he said to send his regards.' The way Ramsey looked at him you'd think Terry had just uttered the ultimate blasphemy. Ramsey completely ignored him, turned on his heels and walked in the opposite direction – he didn't want to know about old Sid from Dagenham. The last thing he needed was a player in the team to remind everyone he once lived in Dagenham! 'I can remember him when greyhounds was growlers,' was one famous remark made about Ramsey.

He did pick Terry twice for his country, two draws against Belgium and Holland. He would have been in a third time had Docherty not chose that exact moment to drop him from Chelsea's first team.

As I said, with Tom it was honeymoon or the divorce court, and Terry had plenty of both in his time at Stamford Bridge. One minute he was captain of the League Cup winning team that beat Leicester on aggregate 3–2 over two legs, the next he wasn't even in the side. It was astonishing behaviour for a man in charge of one of the brightest young teams in the country.

The night Chelsea won the Cup we went back to a big reception. The players and their families were well treated and looked after and we had a great night. A few of the lads had their own parties going on after the reception ended, and none of us got back home until the early hours of the morning. Terry was one of the heroes that night, the captain of the club and scorer of one of the goals that helped them lift the trophy. Seeing him get his medal will go down as one of the greatest memories of my life, yet you couldn't help but wonder if Docherty would find some way to ruin it. Of course he did. The famous night in Blackpool, when eight of Chelsea's first-team squad were sent home for misbehaving, was only a month away.

4

Now let's get one thing straight. Terry wasn't then, and
has never been since, a big boozer. I've told you he was the
orangeade kid until his late teens, and even when he had
made the Chelsea first-team he restricted his drinking to the
occasional beer with the lads. He also had a steady girlfriend,
Christine, back in London who eventually became his wife.
Yet to see Terry and the other seven Chelsea players arrive
back in London by train after Docherty had sent them home
for late night boozing, you'd have thought they were the great
train robbers. I turned on the television and there they all
were, Terry, Marvin Hinton, Barry Bridges, George Graham,
Eddie McCreadie, John Hollins, Bert Murray and Joe
Fascione, with cameras and newspaper men chasing them
down the platform.

It was soon after this that the phone rang at Bonham Road
late on Friday night, and I answered. 'It's Tommy Docherty,'

said the voice. 'Tell Terry he's not playing tomorrow, and he's not captain any more.' That was it. No thank you for the job you've done, no explanation – you're out of the side and stripped of the captaincy, that was how Tom saw fit to break the news. It devastated me, so you can imagine how Terry must have felt when I told him. He was already upstairs in bed asleep, mistakenly preparing for the following day's game.

It's frustrating to look back at those pictures of Terry at Chelsea, seeing the faces of all his team-mates and friends, knowing how it all turned out. Chelsea was his first real love, and he would have stayed there forever had the circumstances been different. Terry met some of his best mates in football through his early days at Chelsea. Allan Harris, for instance, became Terry's assistant manager at a string of clubs, and George Graham was his best man when he married Christine on 3 April 1966. It's funny that they should both have finished up managing the two top London clubs, Spurs and Arsenal, because they have been big mates almost from the day they met.

George was one of Docherty's first signings at Chelsea, he snapped him up from Aston Villa when he was only a teenager. He arrived at the club very quiet and shy, and Docherty used to tease him unmercifully. 'You were doomed, George, until I rescued you from Villa,' he'd say, 'doomed.' He said it so often the players nicknamed him 'Doomed George', a tag he hated. No sooner had he arrived he was placed on a first-team trip to Sweden with the rest of the chaps, none of whom knew him from Adam.

George was a funny lad, a bit of a smoothie and a big Frank Sinatra fan – he had every album the man had made. But as the new boy he kept quiet until the second night away, when the boys were allowed to go out on the town in Gothenburg. They were in a train compartment singing songs and joking about, when suddenly George piped up, in a deep baritone: 'We seem like passing strangers now, funny how things can change,' and the rest of the lads were looking round, staring over their shoulders, thinking 'who's this new boy, who does he think he is.' They let him go right through the song, every verse, until he ended to total silence and Terry said: 'Well that's great for Sarah Vaughan, George, now give us Billy Eckstine!' But it had broken the ice, and everyone took a liking to George except for one man, reserve team goalkeeper John Dunn – and that was down to me.

When Terry first signed for Chelsea, Ted Drake had asked me to keep an eye out for any talent I might see in my area, and Dunn was my one and only success. A friend had recommended him to me, and he had been taken onto the staff at Chelsea as cover for Peter Bonetti. But for some reason Dunn took an instant dislike to George the moment he saw him, and, Terry tells me, spent the rest of the trip to Sweden poking him in the chest, trying to aggravate him.

Trouble between those lads was very rare, they were a good-natured bunch most of the time and Eddie McCreadie was great fun to be with. One day, when Chelsea were staying in a hotel, there was a chap trying to annoy them by making a noise outside their bedroom windows, and Terry couldn't stand it any more. He came to the window and started having a go back, but still the bloke wouldn't leave him alone. In the end, Terry got so frustrated he dropped his trousers and stuck his backside out of the window. Terry always jokes that the fella shouted: 'Don't worry, I'll get you too, Eddie McCreadie!'

The fun the team had together, and the great football they played, made it all the more upsetting that Terry should leave on such a sour note. Once Terry had left, I can't remember speaking a civil word to Tommy Docherty, even to this day. Only a short while ago, a friend of mine called me on a carphone, and we were having a friendly chat. 'I've got an old mate of yours here who would like a word,' he said, 'it's Tommy Docherty.' 'Don't bother,' I told him, 'I don't want to know.'

Another time I was going into a match at Charlton and he was standing by the gate. 'Hello Fred,' he said, as if we were the best mates in the world. 'Sod off, Tom,' I replied, 'people will think you know me.' I'll make no secret of it, I've got no time for the man. What he did at Chelsea was a mistake, and I'm sure now even he knows that. In April 1966, just a few weeks after Terry's wedding, he brought almost a year of uncertainty to an end by telling Terry he could leave Chelsea. The club had been beaten in an FA Cup semi-final, and it was almost as if Docherty was blaming Terry and three other players who were also sold. Barry Bridges, Bert Murray and George Graham all went – it was Docherty's first step towards dismantling the side, and he did it in what seemed to be a fit of pique. Terry played his last game for the club, strangely enough, in a Fairs Cup tie at Barcelona's Nou Camp stadium, where he would one day become a successful manager.

I suppose Terry jumped from the frying pan into the fire with his £80,000 move to Tottenham that year, although his problems this time were with the fans, not the manager. In fact, I took the phone call from Tottenham's boss, Bill Nicholson, that opened the new chapter in his career. It was in the new house Terry and Christine had bought at Beechwood Gardens, Barkingside. Docherty came on first to speak to Terry and tell him of the interest from Spurs and West Ham. Bill Nicholson then phoned and I answered. 'I want to know if Terry would be interested in joining Tottenham,' he said. 'Interested,' I thought, 'he'll be bloody delighted!' Terry spoke to Nicholson for a short while, and no sooner had the phone gone down when it rung again.

'Hello Mr Nicholson,' said Terry. 'Hello Terry,' said the voice, 'it's Ron Greenwood.' Apparently, Docherty had accepted offers from both Spurs and West Ham and it was up to Terry to choose between the two. It was like having a fifteen-year-old son again with the big clubs chasing him, you almost expected old Jimmy Thompson to emerge from the bathroom, to try to persuade him to stay at Chelsea! After speaking to both managers that day, he finally plumped for Spurs and went straight into the team. Within a week he was on a club tour visiting places like Bermuda, San Francisco and Mexico. Following the shattering disillusionment of life under Docherty, it looked as if Terry's year was going to end all right after all.

The record books show that Terry's first year at White Hart Lane went swimmingly. Spurs reached the FA Cup Final against, of all clubs, Chelsea and revenge was sweet as they won 2–1 with Docherty sitting tight-lipped on the bench. It was a great day for Terry, desperate to put one over on Tom who had constantly been sniping at him throughout the season. Docherty claimed Terry was past his best, having peaked at Chelsea. He made a big show of praising his new signing Charlie Cooke, and described Terry as a big fish in a small pool during his time at Stamford Bridge. It made Tottenham's 2–1 victory doubly pleasing to think of Docherty having to explain away his comments to the papers after the match.

However, deep down, Terry had a problem at Spurs. The fans didn't like him, and resented him being talked of as a replacement for John White, the White Hart Lane hero who had been struck by lightning playing golf and had died so tragically. It was unfair on Terry from the start, because no player can ever be a replacement for someone else. There will only ever be one John White, as there will only be one Terry Venables. But the fans didn't see it like that, they seemed to think that to praise Terry would be in some way disrespectful to White's memory, and for the first time in his life he got stick from the fans. I would be sitting in the stand and they'd start hollering and shouting insults and abuse at him; they'd pick on me as well as his father. In the first few games it was only a trickle, but by the middle of the season the criticism had become so bad I was quite shaken by it. I used to get involved in arguments there with the people around me – it was hard not to hit back when you see your son being vilified like that. I knew it was affecting Terry's game as well. He didn't have the same confidence. He was trying to be the player they wanted him to be, not the player he was. I tried to understand how they felt, having a beautiful player like John White snatched from their hands so suddenly, but it was no use. So much of the criticism was unfair, and so few of the fans gave Terry a chance you couldn't help feeling bitter about it. At one stage it was very hard for me to go to watch him play, because I would get so hot under the collar. Some people have no respect for your feelings, and there was one man in particular who had a great big mouth and sat near me; he never left Terry alone. It was Venables this and Venables that all the way through the game.

A few seasons later Terry was playing for Queens Park Rangers at Spurs on Boxing Day and he had a brilliant game. I was sitting with my QPR scarf round my neck, when this bloke started up. 'There we are,' he said, 'look at Venables, we sold a player like that and look what he's doing to us now. What sort of management is that?' I couldn't resist it. I rounded on him and said: 'Hold on, you were always slagging him off when he was here. You hated him, you were worse than anybody.' 'Oh, hello Fred,' he said, embarrassed and trying to be friendly. 'Don't give me that,' I told him, 'people like you made his life a misery at Spurs, and now you want him back ... that's typical.' By now everyone in the stand was looking at us, and he didn't know what to say. Terry would have told me not to get involved, but I had to say my piece, some of what had gone on was scandalous.

Terry was never a man to cry on your shoulder. You could see it affected him, but he wouldn't complain. 'They pay their money, dad,' was all you'd get out of him. 'I don't like it, but what can I do?' Bill Nicholson was very supportive, always telling Terry to forget about it, telling him he was doing a good job.

Nicholson could be a tough guy when he wanted to be, but deep down he was likeable, and he knew how to handle things at a club as big as Tottenham. He worked well with the Press and much of Tottenham's good public image was down to him, and he had a rapport with both players and directors without ever seeming false. I liked Bill, and I know Terry admired his honesty. Spurs was a very different club to Chelsea, though, and players' families weren't made to feel so involved. Nicholson, and the chairman, were people you saw from afar, not people who would approach you for a chat. You drank tea, no alcohol, out of bone china cups in the Oak Room at White Hart Lane and guests were left very much to themselves. I would never say that Spurs were an unfriendly club, except for their supporters at the time, but it was obvious Terry couldn't stay there much longer.

The season before he left, the criticism was really bad in one match against Manchester City. It was an icy pitch and he couldn't do anything right. They were on him from the start, and by the end of the match he looked haunted. A friend told him to go out, get drunk and forget about it, but Terry went straight home. You could see he had about as much as he could take.

That summer he was sold to Queens Park Rangers, managed by our mate from Dagenham, Les Allen, for £70,000 – only £10,000 less than Spurs had paid for him.

41

Rangers were in Division Two, but I was just glad to see him out of the White Hart Lane firing line. It was a clean break, and what was the point of going out every week knowing you had to play out of your skin just to shut the fans up? I felt sorry for Terry, because a lot of people thought it was the end of his career in Division One, but it turned out to be a great move for him.

5

*A*fter the turmoil of his three years at Tottenham, Queens Park Rangers was just what the doctor ordered for Terry. Les Allen had known him since he was a schoolboy in short trousers, playing with a tennis ball under streetlamps in Bonham Road. They liked each other, and the atmosphere off the field was a lot more relaxed. Terry and Christine lived in Loughton now, with their two young daughters Nancy and Tracy, and he'd drive every morning from their home to the club training ground in Ruislip, Middlesex. The club had just been relegated to the Second Division, and many thought it was a comedown for him after the glamorous life at Spurs, but just one look at Terry would tell you it was one of the best things ever to happen to him.

I think his experiences at Tottenham had come as a shock, after eight years of near-constant success with Chelsea. He has never forgotten the time when he walked into a bar and a mate, who couldn't stop buying him drinks when he was an England man and captain at Stamford Bridge, turned his back and ignored him – just because he wasn't the star of the show at Spurs. He had lost a lot of his strength of character, the stuff that made teachers single him out as a leader even as a small boy. But now it was back, in the quiet, relaxed atmosphere at QPR, away from the spotlight and the pressure.

When Les left QPR to be replaced by Gordon Jago, Terry carried on playing at his best. I'd say some of his finest performances were in the blue and white hooped strip of Rangers and it's just a shame there were not more people around to witness them. New boss Jago built one of the liveliest dressing-rooms in the country, not that some of the players needed much encouraging. At his first team-meeting, Rodney Marsh strolled up and told him: 'I'd like you to know, boss, that the players are all fifty per cent behind you!' Jago was a good manager and in 1973 Rangers were promoted to the First Division as runners-up. They were a smashing team to watch, with Marsh and Stan Bowles, two of the game's great crowd-pleasers, Frank McLintock, a double-winning captain with Arsenal in 1971, and brilliant youngsters including Gerry Francis, a future captain of England. They were football's Crazy Gang before Wimbledon were even heard of, and some of the stunts were unbelievable.

At an airport one day, Terry pretended to be a customs official. He stood behind this table, looking very serious and when three American women came through stopped them and asked if they would empty their bags. He must have seemed very convincing, because everything came out, before Terry said 'thank you very much' and walked away! Terry Mancini once took the field with a wig covering his bald head, and it wasn't until the end of the game that he whipped it off to reveal his true identity. Terry, nicknamed 'Henry' after the composer, was the very cockney Londoner, who suddenly found himself playing for the Republic of Ireland because of parentage. In his first international, he patiently stood to attention as the band went through the national anthems. 'This one's a bit boring,' whispered Henry to a team-mate, 'and it goes on for ages. What's ours like?' 'Shut up, you clot,' came the reply, 'this is ours!'

Terry (Venables, that is) even became a TV star the year Rangers returned to Division One. A Big Match camera panned in on him during a match at Derby, and for a bit of fun he wiggled his eyebrows up and down – an old trick he'd been doing since a kid. For some reason it caught the imagination of the public and the TV people put it in the opening sequence of the show. He had newspaper men and photographers going after him for months, and every time he turned around someone was waiting to snap him with a camera, or shouting 'wiggle your eyebrows, Tel!' He was even nominated as sportsman of the month – for juggling his eyebrows it seemed ridiculous. He was the backbone, the brains, the midfield general of a successful QPR team, but two seconds of fun for the cameras was getting him more attention than anything else in his playing career. I don't think Terry minded the sudden, superficial glamour but it did sum up the way that football had changed from the days when men like Ted Drake ruled the roost. You could hardly imagine old Ted wiggling his eyebrows for the man from *The Sun*, but it was now all part of modern day football.

Jago loved it. He had a talent for public relations, and he enjoyed the fact that his lads were getting a lot of the attention. Queens Park Rangers had always been one of the poor relations in London, overshadowed by clubs like Spurs, Arsenal and West Ham. Yet suddenly they were getting the lion's share of attention. All the players had such individual personalities it was obvious the media men would go for them, and they played football with a smile. Terry used to say to Stan Bowles 'go on, show them a few tricks' and Stan would always oblige. Terry would tell me: 'We'll end up playing in cemeteries unless people try to put some fun back into the game.'

I think that's why he gets on so well with Paul Gascoigne at Tottenham these days. Gazza plays football with a smile on his face, he's cocky and confident and Terry appreciates that. Not every manager in the League would have wanted to take a chance on him, but Terry could see there was the talent there from the start. Of course he has to have the occasional word and maybe settle him down, but Terry likes strong characters, people who can have a laugh and joke and lift the spirit in the dressing-room. Someone like Gazza would have fitted in perfectly at QPR, and Terry was really happy there.

By that time I had taken an early retirement from the docks, and myself and Myrtle had bought the Royal Oak public house in Chingford. I suppose Terry's name might have helped us get it, but the money was all our own. We gave up our council house in Bonham Road and paid the £1,700 for the tenancy. By the time we arrived we had sixty pounds left in our pocket, that was all we owned. The place looked a lot different back then, a lot smaller and we didn't have a clue whether we would be able to make it work. Myrtle had experience of running a business through the café in Dagenham, but it was still one hell of a gamble.

Terry would pop in to see us every day, first on his way to Tottenham, then later when he moved to QPR. He used to come past here on his way from their training ground to his home in the prime part of Loughton, and he always stopped by for lunch. We spent almost every Sunday together, and I can honestly say I've rarely seen him happier. He was once again winning rave reviews for his performances on the field, even though he'll be the first to admit that, at thirty, his level of fitness had probably peaked. He'd tell Gerry Francis and Martyn Busby: 'You're the legs and I'm the brains,' and they were an excellent combination.

That is why I have never been able to understand Jago's sudden decision to transfer him to Crystal Palace in September, 1974. It was like a rerun of what had happened at Chelsea, although I would never compare Jago in any other way to Docherty. Stan Bowles and Terry Mancini were already on the transfer list, and suddenly Terry was off to Palace as part of a swop deal for Don Rogers. Terry was very upset about what happened, and the players were furious. He was their captain and they looked up to him, he was the man they expected to lead their challenge for some of the top trophies in the game. But Jago thought he knew best, and Terry was on his way again, to the London club that would launch his career in management.

Palace were in Division Three at the time, but they had one very important attraction for Terry – their manager, Malcolm Allison. The pair had first met when Terry was fourteen and Malcolm was one of the men West Ham sent round to persuade him to go to Upton Park. He was very flamboyant even then, with a love of a good night out and life in the fast lane. These days, a champagne lifestyle is not so uncommon amongst managers, but in 1957 Malcolm stood out from the crowd. Terry took a shine to him straight away, and he said his coaching was so inventive and interesting, and so different from the rest.

Malcolm came as close as anyone to persuading Terry to turn down Chelsea as a schoolboy, and fifteen years later the pair had eventually teamed up. To a certain extent they had never been away. Even when Terry was at Chelsea, Spurs and QPR, Malcolm was always one of the men he stayed close to. They would often meet up in London to discuss

47

football, and Terry had often spoken of his admiration for Malcolm's ideas and original approach. It didn't matter that Palace were in Division Three, he wanted to work with Malcolm but even Terry couldn't have predicted how quickly his life was to change.

Terry only played fourteen games for Palace before he was struck down with a heel injury. The doctor diagnosed it as arthritis, and insisted it wasn't wise for him to continue playing. At the time, it could have been a disaster, but Malcolm had other plans. He invited Terry on to the staff as coach, the first step on the management ladder that would take Terry back to Queens Park Rangers, over to Barcelona and then finally back to Tottenham. Allison, the master coach and tactician, had obviously seen something in Terry which other managers had failed to spot. He wasn't scared of the influence Terry could have on a team, and the pair of them worked together to give Crystal Palace a season they would never forget. Malcolm and Terry would spend hours mapping out how to make the next day's training interesting for the team. They'd have it all planned out: different ideas, different experiments so that no-one would ever get bored. I'd watch from the touchline baffled by some of what went on, but they understood each other and the players seemed to love it.

Their first full season in charge began with Palace still in Division Three, but ended just ninety minutes away from Wembley. Malcolm and Terry guided them through to an FA Cup semi-final against Southampton – one of only a handful of lower division sides ever to make that stage. With two such colourful characters in charge the Press couldn't get enough of them. I'm sure everyone remembers the pictures of Malcolm in his fedora hat and big cigar taking the applause of the crowd that day. He was a real rascal, and always knew how to get attention for himself, the club and its players. I can remember seeing a photograph of the team, dressed in

1930s-style pinstripe suits and carrying violin cases, looking like extras from a Jimmy Cagney film. The team were young and exciting to watch, and the atmosphere that surrounded them reflected that. A lot of Malcolm's ideas have rubbed off on Terry, and they are still in touch to this day. Terry will always contact Malcolm for advice, or just a chat. At the age of sixty, he's still as flamboyant as ever and full of mischief but the nights out are rarer than in his younger days.

Malcolm has been a massive influence on Terry's career as a manager, and his departure in summer 1976 left the way clear for Terry to take over. Palace, unfortunately, lost their semi-final to Southampton, and missed out on the chance of becoming the only Third Division side in the competition ever to reach Wembley. They also missed out on promotion to the Second Division that year, and chairman Ray Bloye offered Terry the chance to take over as manager. It was uncanny. Myrtle had always maintained that Terry would one day be a football manager, right from his earliest days in the game. She points to a piece of schoolwork when he was very young, again talking about his ambitions: 'I want to play for Tottenham, and manage Tottenham.' Well, the post at White Hart Lane was still over eleven years away, but in the meantime Crystal Palace would do nicely and Terry accepted at once.

He was very young, just thirty-three, but I don't think he gave that a thought. Throughout his career Terry has always been one step ahead of the game: in Chelsea's team at sixteen-and-a-half, the only man to represent England at every level, and now one of the youngest-ever managers of a football club – it was some challenge. Terry met Bloye and agreed he would succeed Malcolm as manager, and then the most astonishing thing happened – Arsenal announced they also wanted him to take charge. It was an incredible situation for a young man to be in; he'd never been more than a coach at

Palace, yet suddenly one of the biggest clubs in the world wanted to take him straight from Division Three, and put him in the manager's chair. A lot of people would have walked straight back into Bloye's office and said 'thanks, but goodbye', but Terry was different. I think he almost fainted when he heard of Arsenal's interest in him, but he was equally adamant that he couldn't let Palace down. 'I've given my word,' he said, 'I've got to stick with it.'

I think Terry had seen so much double-dealing in football that he was determined not to start the wrong way. Arsenal might have offered a short cut to the top, but Terry refused to be compromised. 'What I might lose in the short term, I think I'll get back in the long term,' he said, and I think he has been proved right. People respected that decision, and I think it boosted the morale of the players at Crystal Palace to see that show of commitment from their manager.

That season proved to be the greatest start Terry could have had in management. After the disappointments of the previous year, Palace were promoted to the Second Division with a team many were already tipping for the top. Terry learnt from his days at Chelsea, and built a team with a strong spirit, and an emphasis on youth. Kenny Sansom, who went on to play over eighty games for England was at left-back, and Terry stood by other promising teenagers including Vince Hilaire and Jerry Murphy. Sometimes it would prove difficult for them to adapt to first-team football, but he would always show faith and give them a run of games in the first-team to help build confidence. On the return trip from away matches, the jacket would come off and he would be up the back of the coach, drinking lager, smoking cigars and cracking jokes with the rest of the team – but there was never any question of who was boss. The players respected Terry for his coaching, and his loyalty to them when it would have been so easy for him to up and leave for Arsenal.

The mood at the club was always optimistic and relaxed, and much of that was down to Terry's careful preparation. Every morning he would talk to a tape recorder during his hour's drive from Loughton to Palace's ground, coming up with different schemes and training methods. He installed Allan Harris, a close friend and business partner since their days together at Chelsea, as his assistant at Selhurst Park. Together they would work on the schedules, the way that Terry and Malcolm once had, and after just a year in the Second Division the hard graft again paid off.

On 11 May 1979, Palace beat Burnley 2–0 to come roaring back into the First Division as champions. It was a magnificent night for us all. I couldn't believe it when I arrived at Selhurst Park, there were over 50,000 fans at a ground that had once been half-empty. It must have been a special atmosphere because even Terry was nervous. He told me later he had got goose pimples just hearing the roar of the crowd as Palace took the field. The atmosphere was tense with the score 0–0 at half-time, and Palace had to wait until almost the last ten minutes before scoring twice – what a feeling that was! Sitting in the stands I couldn't believe my boy had done it. He'd been a manager just three seasons, and he'd taken a club through two Divisions. They were already being called 'the team of the eighties' because many of their players were so young and so talented, and the scorers that night, Ian Walsh and Dave Swindlehurst, were both players Terry had shown faith in throughout his time at the club.

It was a night for celebration, and there were parties going on all over the place. I couldn't help but feel sorry for Billy Elliott, the manager of Sunderland, whose side would have won promotion if Palace had failed. He was sitting in the stand near me, and he looked absolutely choked when Palace's goals went in. It was one of those astonishing games – defeat we stayed down, draw we won promotion, but the victory meant the Championship! Brighton, who would have taken the title had we not got all the points, heard the news from the captain of their aeroplane, as they flew to America for a club tour.

It had been a great year in every way for Terry. His success with Palace had persuaded Ron Greenwood to make him part of the England set-up, and he was given the task of coaching the under-21s with Dave Sexton. I went on many of the trips at Terry's invitation and would fly all over the world to watch the young England boys in action. I became something of a jet-setter in those days. That was another personal triumph for Terry – to be involved at that level after such a short time in management. Most men have to wait the best part of a lifetime before getting a call from England, Terry had been a manager less than three years. John Cartwright, the man who had brought many of Palace's stars through from a young age was also honoured and given the job as England's youth team boss. All this in one season of football and the next promised to be just as exciting.

It didn't take long for Palace to hit the headlines again. Only two months into their first season in Division One, a 4–1 win over Ipswich saw them go top and it looked as if their rise and rise would be irresistible. But all good things have to come to an end, and I think the newly-tagged 'team of the eighties' found the step up a bit tougher than expected, and they eventually finished mid-table.

Now was the time to do some serious thinking. Players like Murphy, Hilaire, Peter Nicholas and Billy Gilbert had seen them through three divisions, but it was obvious that survival was going to take a bit more and that is how Terry became involved in one of the most incredible transfer deals of all time. Arsenal's manager Terry Neill had paid one million pounds for Queens Park Rangers striker Clive Allen at the end of the previous season, but having got him to

Highbury found he didn't quite fit in. Clive, son of Les, was not going to be in the starting line-up for Arsenal's first game, and Neill had now turned his attentions to Terry's left-back at Palace, Kenny Sansom. Between them, the managers struck up a deal. Arsenal would get Sansom, and in exchange Clive comes to Palace as probably the only million pound player never to make an appearance for his club!

When Terry met Clive at a club in London the poor lad obviously couldn't believe what was happening to him. With a bit of persuasion Terry clinched the deal, and Clive signed the next day at the Hilton Hotel. Terry also bought a goalkeeper, Paul Barron, from Arsenal for an extra £300,000. It all seemed so simple at the time, but the next day there was one hell of a fuss. MPs raised questions in Parliament about levying a tax on transfers of more than £100,000, and Arsenal came in for a lot of criticism. Terry couldn't understand what the fuss was about. He'd simply swopped one good player for another one; the only money that had changed hands was for Barron, the goalkeeper. But the controversy raged in the papers for days.

It wasn't long before Terry himself was to be on the move, back to the club where he had experienced five years as a player – Queens Park Rangers. It was another figure from his past, Tommy Docherty, who was sacked to make way for Terry at Loftus Road. The only sour note in the whole affair came when people accused Terry of walking out on Palace in a time of need. I know that was not the case. Palace had started the season badly, and when Terry heard of QPR's offer his first reaction was to tell Ray Bloye he was prepared to stay. 'I'll only go if you can agree compensation for me,' he said; and Bloye did.

It would have been easy for Palace to keep Terry, all they had to say was that compensation couldn't be agreed. Instead, Terry found out they had approached two other managers behind his back, before asking him if he wanted to stay on. It was poor reward for the loyalty he had shown them four years earlier, when he had the chance to go to Arsenal, but it gave Terry the chance to work with a man who has since become one of his closest friends, Rangers chairman Jim Gregory.

6

Terry and England's former under-21 manager Dave Sexton are members of a very select club – they are the only managers to leave the employ of Jim Gregory at Queens Park Rangers of their own free will. Jim is a notorious figure in football, ask anybody and they'll tell you the same thing: 'He's the chairman who sacks all the managers.' Yet he and Terry got on like a house on fire almost from the word go. Terry found that although Jim has high standards and insists on them at all times, he always let him get on with the job of managing the football club. He didn't interfere in the day-to-day running of the side, and Terry always knew he could go into Jim's office to discuss a particular problem. Jim would listen and give advice, but he left Terry to be his own man, which is more than you can say about a number of modern-day chairmen.

People always talk of Jim as a slippery character, as if he

was in some way dishonest. I always found him to be the complete opposite. Sure, Jim was a good schemer, he understood business as all successful men do, and could size up a situation or a person very quickly. But he wasn't tricky with money, and at Queens Park Rangers he always insisted the bills were paid on time. Jim would go mad at the people in the office if he ever received a phone call from another club or person claiming he owed them money. He was meticulous in his business dealings, and always insisted debts were met to the hour. To hear him talk you knew he wasn't the sort of bloke who would forget to date a cheque to buy him an extra four days time, or phone you to claim he was about to post it when the wind took it away. Because he was straight like that Jim wanted it both ways, and he had no hesitation in bringing the lawyers in if someone was late with a payment.

I got on with Jim from the first time I met him, and he and Terry made a great team. They were both characters, a couple of rascals together, and struck up the instant rapport Terry had only previously found with men like Malcolm Allison. I often used to sit near Jim in the directors box at Queens Park Rangers, and I can remember the day he saved me from being thrown out. I'll confess I'm not usually the quietest man in the posh seats at football, and sometimes I find it hard to keep control. I'm always shouting out and having a go, and I've never been the greatest fan of referees and linesmen.

This day we were playing Blackburn Rovers in a Second Division match, and they were awarded a goal that wasn't. It was the strangest thing, the ball came in from the left, seemed to hit the bar, came out to one of their players who headed it into the net. But something about the sequence of events wasn't right – the ball had rebounded back from where it came. Something had to be up, because that was defying the laws of physics. If the ball hits the bar, it rebounds at a right angle. We all knew something was wrong, but no-one could work out what, and then it struck me. The ball had hit one of the net supports, it hadn't hit the bar at all, it had gone over the bar, out of play and then come back in – the goal should be disallowed. Terry must have realized this at the same time, because suddenly he began protesting furiously to the referee from the dug-out, and all hell was let loose. The referee consulted his linesman, decided the goal was good, and pointed to the centre circle for a restart.

Meanwhile, I had got into an almighty row with the man sitting opposite me and, I admit, completely lost my rag. I was swearing and cursing at this bloke with a Bill Haley kiss curl, who was getting very upset. Just my luck, it was the chairman of Blackburn Rovers and now the President of the Football League, Bill Fox. Obviously upset, he rounded on Jim Gregory: 'This man has been swearing at me,' he said, 'it's an improper way to behave and I want you to do something about it.' Everyone looked at Jim to see what he would do, and I really felt I had put my foot in it. 'If you don't like it,' he told Fox, '*you* can leave.' Good old Jim was more concerned that we had been done out of this goal than any offence I might have caused to the visiting chairman.

Fox looked furious. I was in a bit of a state myself, and at the end of the game I marched straight into the directors lounge for some refreshment, still angry over what I thought was blatant injustice. As I always do, when annoyed, I made straight for the cake tray, picked up a chocolate éclair and bit into it as hard as I could. Everyone watched as the cream flew out of the end, performed a neat arc and landed slap on Bill Fox's suit. It was like a slow-motion replay as it made its journey down his lapel, you couldn't help laughing. Jim thought it was hysterical, but I've always steered clear of the directors box since when Blackburn have been playing.

That's not the only time I've got myself into trouble at football matches. Only a short while ago I was watching

Tottenham play, and England's ex-manager Bobby Robson was in the stand. At the time there was a lot of controversy over Robson's attitude towards Spurs's hero Paul Gascoigne, and as I was leaving the ground a man shouted to Robson: 'What are you messing Gazza about for, Robson. Why don't you leave him alone!' I didn't think anything of it, but Robson suddenly rounded on me. 'Did you hear that,' he said, 'and I bet you agree with him.' 'It's nothing to do with me, Bobby,' I said, 'it's none of your business what I think; the man is talking to you.'

Jim Gregory was nobody's fool and I rate him as one of the most knowledgeable chairmen I've ever met. He was also such a shrewd businessman – a self-made millionaire from the most ordinary of backgrounds – who made a fortune selling cars. I think people just liked to label him as a 'second-hand car salesman', and never looked any further than that. It's a shame because Jim made Queens Park Rangers a force in football again, thanks to many clever business dealings when Terry was at the club. Of course, Terry bought and sold the right players, but Jim was always in the background to make sure the price was good. Jim liked Terry, and he liked the sort of football Terry produced at QPR.

When he arrived there they had been struggling in the Second Division, but once again, Terry turned the club around. He spent his first season nurturing talent including Terry Fenwick, Gary Waddock, Simon Stainrod and Glenn Roeder, and in the close season bought Clive Allen back from Crystal Palace for £400,000. But it was another incident that made the headlines that summer – QPR's decision to install League football's first artificial pitch.

Jim and Terry went to Canada to look at surfaces used for sport in that country, and came back with plans to lay a substance called omniturf at Loftus Road. It must have been a strange feeling for Terry, the man who had written a book called *They Used To Play On Grass*, life imitating art. I've still got a piece of the ill-fated omniturf at home, collected when it was finally torn up three years ago and sold off in bits as souvenirs. But at the time the reasoning behind it was simple. Plastic was a consistent all-year-round surface, which grass is not, and could be played on in all weathers. If someone came to you and offered to sell you a pitch that would be perfect in August, then slow and heavy in December, then bone hard with the ball bouncing all over the place in April, you'd refuse. Yet that, argued Terry, is what ninety-nine per cent of English pitches are like. Plastic was a way of ensuring consistency, it never varied whether football was played in a drought or a snowstorm. It could be hired out privately when not in use by the football club, something no team would dare do to their own grass surface for fear of damaging it, and there would never be the worry of a game being postponed because of bad weather. Plastic would survive even the fiercest English winter.

The arguments were fine in practice, but as soon as the rest of the ninety-one clubs had a look at it, all hell was let loose. Terry and Jim were banging their heads against a brick wall if they thought anyone else was going to accept their baby without a fuss. Clubs claimed they would be at a disadvantage coming to Loftus Road for one match a season, and that Rangers would be better prepared. They ignored the fact that QPR had twenty-one games away from home, on grass – who would be at a disadvantage then? Rangers always gave the opposition use of the surface on the Friday before a game to get them acclimatized, anyway a lot of clubs used all-weather training pitches to keep them going through the winter months.

In the end, I think Terry got tired of defending it. He never mentioned how much harder it was to train players to perform on plastic, coaching them in the one-touch football that was needed. No-one took the laid-back attitude of the American football player Joe Namath who, when asked if he preferred grass to astroturf, replied: 'Don't know. Ain't never smoked no astroturf!' The League reluctantly accepted QPR's new pitch, but the FA weren't so sure. They were considering making QPR play any home FA Cup games on neutral ground, until Jim stepped in and told them he'd pull Rangers out of the competition rather than do that. Finally, with hours to spare, the FA relented and QPR went on to reach the Final that season!

Terry had already been to Wembley as a player, but seeing him take the field ahead of a long line of his QPR players is a magnificent memory. The road to the Final hadn't been easy. The first game was a home tie against First Division Middlesbrough and Rangers started as favourites because of the artificial pitch. The game ended in a 1–1 draw, then QPR won on Ayresome Park's grass 3–2 after extra time. So much for the plastic advantage. The next two ties against Blackpool and Notts County were won comfortably, and then Terry was drawn against his former club Crystal Palace in the quarter-finals. It was a big day for both Terry and Clive Allen, his new striker, because of past connections with Selhurst Park, and Clive took great delight in scoring the winner. Another goal from Clive settled the semi-final with West Brom and then it was on to Wembley, and Keith Burkinshaw's Tottenham.

Every time I go back to Wembley, the memories of that and all the other great days come flooding back. I can't choose between them – Terry's first appearance there as an England schoolboy against Scotland, his first full England international against Belgium in 1965, the FA Cup Final with Tottenham and beating Chelsea 2–1, or seeing him walk out in his smart suit at the head of a bunch of players he had taken from nowhere and turned into a force to be reckoned with. I still have the picture on the wall of my pub of the teams lining up, but unfortunately victory that day was not to be. Terry Fenwick equalized Tottenham's Glenn Hoddle goal to take the game into a replay, but on that Thursday night I saw Terry lose at Wembley for the first time in my life. Rangers were without Clive Allen this time, and Glenn Roeder was suspended – a goal from Glenn Hoddle settled it. The post-match club function was such an anti-climax after all the hopes and dreams that had gone before, but we all knew Rangers would come good again and the next season they did us proud.

By the time the 1982–3 season started I think Terry had proved beyond doubt that he could manage even at the highest level. Reaching the FA Cup Final with Rangers was a great achievement, and he had also coached England's under-21 side to success in the European Championships. They had beaten Poland over two legs to reach the final against Scotland, and they held on for a draw, after winning the first leg 1–0, to lift the trophy. Players including Steve McMahon, Mark Hateley, Gary Mabbutt, Terry Fenwick and Sammy Lee all went on to play successfully for their country at full level, and there is no doubt in my mind at all that Terry in some way helped their careers.

However, his first duty was to Rangers, and he worked long and hard that year to get them back into the First Division. Terry had surrounded himself with a select group of friends from his playing days, who coached and worked with the players at different levels. Allan Harris remained his assistant, but Frank McLintock came in to run the reserve team and Terry brought George Graham out of retirement to work with the youth side. George had retired, with thoughts of running a pub, until Terry persuaded him to return to football at Loftus Road. It wasn't an act of charity, Terry has always admired George's thoughts on the game, and looking at his recent successses with Arsenal he's proved to be right.

The club had been doing well all season, and it was in the run-in to a match that could clinch the title, against Leeds, that Jim Gregory dropped his biggest bombshell yet. 'I'm selling out of the football club,' he told Terry, 'and I would like you to buy it.' The news came like a bolt from the blue. Manage *and* own your own football club? It was unheard of. Yet the idea appealed to Terry and he set about putting a plan into action. As he told Jim: 'If you are definitely selling-out it might just as well be me in charge as someone I don't get on with. At least I won't have anyone else to blame if something goes wrong.'

On 23 April 1983, QPR beat Leeds 1–0 to clinch promotion to the First Division, and Gregory immediately announced his scheme. He would keep control of Rangers stadium, and Terry would take over as majority shareholder, and boss of the club, on and off the field. Jim had his own ideas: to put a roof over the stadium so it could be used as a multi-purpose venue to stage concerts and big shows.

Rangers were crowned Second Division champions at the end of that season, ten points ahead of second-placed Wolves, and fifteen clear of third placed Leicester. Terry took the fans' applause in the last home game as manager.

When the following season began, the plan was halfway complete, with Terry as managing director and owner of the second largest share interest in Queens Park Rangers. His days were always full. He would go into the training ground in the morning to coach and work with the team, then back to the club offices that afternoon to take charge of business arrangements. It was a lot of work for one man, but it was a dual role that interested Terry.

Throughout his career the job of being just a player or manager has never been enough to fully occupy him, and he has always developed sidelines whether it was writing books or songs, or other business interests. Now he almost had the lot in one job, and he was already planning for the future at QPR. He and Jim schemed to develop the leisure side, and in time they wanted to take on an executive to run the promotion and commercial outlets. But to do that, Rangers had to be established as a successful First Division side and that was Terry's immediate task. He did more than that, taking Rangers into Europe for the first time since 1976. The end-of-season dinner was a happy affair.

Terry looked set for a long and successful stay with Rangers, and we had a lot of fun. I remember joking with Jim Gregory about his driving ability, and he would always claim to be the worst driver in the world. He had a big Rolls-Royce and he would say: 'I've never had an accident, Fred. When people see me coming they know to get out of the way!' We had a lot of laughs together and everyone was on a high because Rangers were going into Europe. What no-one knew at the time was that Terry would be getting there a lot sooner than we all thought.

7

I think one of the secrets of Terry's success in football is that he's always been one step ahead of the game. I'll give you an example. Gordon Williams, Terry's co-author of the Hazell books, tells the story of the night Crystal Palace won promotion to Division One by beating Burnley. The champagne was flowing and everyone was milling about, elated at the team's success. There was a huge crowd whooping it up in Terry's office, but when Gordon tried to seek his mate out for a celebratory pat on the back he was nowhere to be seen. Gordon found him on the fringes of the party, wearing a dark look on his face. 'What are you thinking about?' he asked Terry. 'Next year,' was the reply. That's typical of Terry, and one of the reasons he was so well equipped for the Barcelona job can be found in just that sort of pre-planning.

The first English manager to get the chance to go to Nou

Camp was Bobby Robson in 1982, shortly before he took on the manager's role with England. He turned it down because, he told Terry, he couldn't speak the language. Hearing that, Terry was determined not to be caught out the same way. His idea was to learn a language in the spare time managers and players always get on away trips. Instead of hanging about the hotel or watching TV in his room, Terry buried his nose in a teach-yourself-Spanish book. He'd read it on the team coach as they travelled up the motorway, and any time during the day when he was given a spare minute. His choice of Spanish was simple. Friends said it was one of the easier languages to master, and he spent a lot of time on holiday there – it would come in useful for that if nothing else.

The rumours that Terry knew at the time he was going to Barcelona are simply untrue. It was a happy accident, but the sort that could only happen to a man with the brain to see the possibilities of a career for an English manager abroad. With British club successes in Europe in recent years through Liverpool, Aston Villa and Nottingham Forest it was becoming increasingly obvious that sooner or later the top continental clubs were going to start looking towards Britain for inspiration. Terry was determined to be ready for the challenge.

When he left for Barcelona, on 21 May 1984, I didn't have the slightest idea he was going to get the job. He told me he was one of many managers interviewed, and said: 'I'm only going out to have a look around to see what they have to offer.' I didn't worry too much. He talked about it so breezily, no-one could have predicted our conversation the next time he phoned me. 'I've got the job, dad,' he said from Spain. 'You mean you've really signed for them,' I gasped. 'Yes,' he said, 'don't worry, you'll love it out here. It's not as far away as it seems. You're here in no time. Come over at the weekend and I'll show you around.'

It would be lying to say I wasn't a bit down when I came

off the phone. We had always been so close, round each other's houses, and we always spent Sunday lunchtime together having a quiet drink, just the two of us. I was delighted he had got the job, if that was what he wanted, but miserable at the thought of being separated from my only son.

No-one, not even Terry, had expected the appointment to be so swift. He was one of three managers interviewed for the post, which had been vacated by Argentina's World-Cup winning manager Cesar Menotti, and the competition was fierce to say the least. His rivals were Michel Hidalgo, the manager of the French team that had won the European Championships, and Helmut Benthuaus, who had just won the West German Bundesliga with Stuttgart. In the middle of Terry's interview they had stopped for dinner in a smart banqueting suite at Barcelona's Nou camp stadium. The president of the club, José-Luiz Nunez, was anxious to impress and offered Terry a cigar from a very expensive-looking box. But when he opened the lid he discovered, to his embarrassment, that it was empty. There was an awkward silence and then Terry reached down and produced his own cigar from inside his sock. 'It's the only item of clothing that can be guaranteed not to bend it,' he told Nunez. Everyone laughed, and Terry reckons they gave him the job because of his ingenuity!

I immediately made plans for my own trip to Barcelona, and quickly found it was as easy as he had described. An hour's drive to Gatwick, followed by a nice English breakfast at a hotel near the airport, hop on the plane and no sooner had I read the paper, I was landing in Spain. Barcelona's large airport is only fifteen minutes drive from the centre of town, and I couldn't believe the scenes that greeted my arrival.

All I can say is that the Barcelona journalists must have some very good contacts at the airport, because reporters and photographers were all over the place. I haven't a clue how they knew I was coming, but they were practically waiting on the tarmac for the plane to arrive. My photograph was all over the papers the next day, and I knew then that Terry had taken on one of the biggest jobs in football. Once outside the airport, nothing changed, there were hundreds of cab drivers waiting to take my fare, and all of them seemed to know me. I was astonished. Back home in England the father of a footballer can live out his life in relative obscurity – but in Spain 'Papa Venables' was big, big news.

Meanwhile, in England, it was Terry's sudden departure from Queens Park Rangers that was causing quite a stir. The night the news broke, Jim Gregory, in disbelief, phoned me at the pub. He and Terry had recently fallen out over money, but it was obviously something Jim felt could have been sorted out without Terry leaving. 'He hasn't really signed, has he, Fred?' he asked me. 'I'm afraid so,' I told him, 'you've lost him now.'

Looking around the Catalan capital on my first day I could see how the pull of Barcelona was no match for a rainy day in Shepherd's Bush. Everything about the place was perfect, the weather was warm and sunny, the people were friendly and the lifestyle spectacular. Barcelona, with home gates of 120,000, are one of the richest clubs in the world, and they certainly live up to it. Terry was staying at the Princess Sofia Hotel, a magnificent place overlooking the ground, and you couldn't help but be impressed by the lavish surroundings.

Terry's first job was to convince the fans he was a worthy manager of their club. Menotti had been a World Cup winner ... but Venables? Few fans had ever heard of him. Other Spanish managers were predicting he wouldn't last a year in the job, one even said: 'There are no good English coaches.' Terry's start couldn't have been more controversial.

He was hardly in the job a week when he agreed the

transfer of Diego Maradona to Italian club Napoli for six million pounds. It's wrong to suggest, as some have, that Terry didn't want Maradona at Barcelona. This was a man he had described as 'the best player in the world' and I know he was looking forward to working with him. But Maradona had his own problems at the club. To begin with he was banned from playing until October for starting a brawl in the previous year's Cup Final with Bilbao. When the bid came in from Naples, Terry demanded a quick decision from Barcelona's eighteen-man board, and the deal was allowed to go through. There was no question of a personality clash between the two men – I don't think Diego was at the club long enough for one to happen! If that had heads spinning in Barcelona, Terry's next move was more sensational still. Ignoring Barcelona's taste for big-name, expensive buys, Terry chose as his first signing a little-known Scottish striker called Steve Archibald. Sure, Steve was a household name and a respected striker in Britain, but in Spain he was a nobody. Terry felt he would fit in, and had always admired his goalscoring talent. He first tried to buy him at Crystal Palace, when Steve was coming to England from Aberdeen, but was thwarted when Archibald chose Spurs. Now the pull of Barcelona meant there would be no problem – Terry saw his chance, and took it. 'If he's a loner like they say,' Terry told me at the time, 'then coming to a foreign country won't bother him. You might as well be a loner in Barcelona as London.'

Looking back to Terry's earliest days in Barcelona, I can see a lot of the strength of purpose he inherited from his mother, Myrtle. He showed great single-mindedness in selling an obvious crowd-pleaser like Maradona, and putting Archibald in his place. Few men would have had the courage to do that, but Terry knew then that the stakes were high. Barcelona demanded success or the sack, and if Terry was going to get the sack, he was going to do it his way, and no-one else's.

There is a lot of his late mother in Terry. I'm bold and erratic and I've done all sorts of crazy things in my life, taken chances and risks when I know I shouldn't. But Myrtle would always look at a situation, weigh it up, and once she had made up her mind there was nothing could persuade her to do otherwise. While I schemed and scraped, Myrtle made plans, and I think that's exactly what Terry was doing when he bought Steve Archibald. He saw a man whom he felt could do well at Barcelona and he didn't care what the public or Press reaction would be. I admire him for that, and as we all know it paid off beyond everyone's wildest dreams.

Terry took over as manager officially on 1 July, in front of 60,000 screaming fans at the club's training ground. That attendance seems hard to believe when you consider Manchester United can't attract that number to Old Trafford for a League game, but as I've said, Barcelona is so much bigger than any other club in the world. A crowd of that size turns up to watch the first training session, and they sit in seats as if they were watching a Saturday afternoon game. The manager then has to give a short speech, to introduce himself to the crowd, and I think Terry won a lot of them over that day by speaking in their local dialect, Catalan. The Barcelona region is fiercely independent, they detest Madrid and the rest of Spain, and speak in their own dialect, a strange mixture of French and Spanish.

When Terry first came to the area he couldn't work out why conversations were so difficult for him to understand, despite having learned Spanish. Then he realized everyone spoke Catalan, and he was back to square one. But, in the short space of time since his appointment, Terry had mastered enough of the local language to be able to give his opening address in the dialect of the region, and I think that was his first step towards winning over the doubters. He showed he respected their language, and the crowd went wild. His speech was given favourable reviews on all the TV and radio stations – Señor Venables was a hit!

Which is more than can be said for Papa Venables, after his first night out with the luminaries at Barcelona. It was at a very grand hotel, the Avenue de Palace, and I had no idea that Terry was going to be joined by the entire staff and directors of his new football club. I arrived at the hotel and he said: 'We're just about to have dinner, Fred. Come and join us.' But as soon as I walked through the huge doors and saw the dining area all laid out, I knew I had made a mistake. There were hundreds of knives, forks and spoons and more plates than I had ever seen in my life. The first-team squad were already seated, plus anybody who was anybody at the club, including the team doctor, Nunez and vice-president Nicolau Casaus (a hero in the Catalan region because of his efforts against Franco during the Spanish Civil War).

When the first course arrived, spaghetti bolognaise, I had never seen anything like it, and didn't have a clue how it was meant to be eaten. I had a sneaky look round for clues and saw that my dinner companions were twisting it around their fork, holding it on with the spoon. Terry says you could see the panic on my face there and then, but when mine arrived I was determined to have a go. I twirled it around my fork brought it up to my mouth and just as I was about to bite in, the lot slipped off the end and went straight down my shirt and tie. I felt such a fool, but Terry saw what had happened and told me: 'Don't worry, have another go.' Now, I took a lot more time, very slowly and methodically working it around the fork, deliberately bringing it away from my plate – I really thought I'd mastered the art. But the same thing happened again, and I finished up with another load of spaghetti bolognaise down my shirt. By this stage, Terry was beginning to grimace, and there was only thing left for me to do. I put the spoon and fork down and called the waiter over. 'Take this away,' I told him, 'I don't like it.' 'He doesn't need the plate,' Terry joked, 'he'll eat it off his shirt.'

It would be churlish to complain about the food in Barcelona, because I've never known a city with so many top restaurants. I don't think either I or Terry had a bad meal in all the time we spent there, and some of the fish restaurants were gorgeous. Even the fast food stalls had a different flavour to them. Often we'd stop at a little kiosk in one of Barcelona's wide, busy streets for a hot dog and an ice-cold beer. In that temperature, it went down a treat, and we would stand and watch and let the people go by. A lot of the fans would come up to us, very friendly, with different pronunciations of Venables, all except the right one. 'Ben-a-bless' was the most common, but Terry and I would chat and have a giggle with them. Terry would joke that every time I went out there his weight went up by two stones because of the hot dogs and the beer. 'I was nicely trimmed down before you arrived,' he'd say, 'now look at the state of me.' But it was good to know that he wasn't so far away in real terms.

In fact, I think I would have felt more isolated had he been manager of Rangers in Scotland, or Newcastle United. One of the great advantages of managing in Spain is that you are finished by one o'clock. Spanish clubs don't have managers in the English sense, they have coaches, and the club is run by the directors and administrators. Terry's duties ended with preparing the team for matches and getting results. All contracts, all transfer negotiations were out of his hands. After his managing director's role at Queens Park Rangers it gave him a lot more time to himself. I could arrive in Barcelona at lunch-time, knowing we would have the whole afternoon to ourselves.

Terry's only commitment would be between five and six

o'clock, when he would go for Spanish and Catalan lessons with a local professor. He never missed those lessons, which can often spell the difference between success and failure in a place like Barcelona. Terry's assistant, Allan Harris, who travelled with him from Queens Park Rangers, never got to grips with Spanish as quickly and it must have been difficult for him to communicate with the players through an interpreter at training sessions. Could you imagine, for instance, the players' reaction at Tottenham or Arsenal to a manager who only spoke Spanish? Of course, continental players are more used to foreign coaches, but after a little while they will expect you to know at least the basics of their own language, which in time both Terry and Allan did. I feel Terry's ability to speak Spanish earned him their initial respect and contributed greatly to the club's success in his first season.

I was overawed the first time I was shown around Barcelona's Nou Camp stadium. I had been to Wembley on many occasions, and the other great grounds in England, but nothing compared to this. Film stars could not have received better treatment than Barcelona's players. Once they had finished they hardly had to lift a finger for themselves. In the dressing-rooms every place had a hair dryer and comb laid out for each player, and there were individual showers in a line – and a jacuzzi! The dressing-rooms are all underground, and to the side is a chapel for the Roman Catholic players to say their prayers before a game. Even with 120,000 people in the ground you cannot hear a thing downstairs as it is sound-proofed and separated from the main stadium by huge under-ground car parks.

As I walked to the stadium to watch Terry's new team play their first match I was impressed at how trouble-free and easy it seemed to be for fans to get into the stadium. Most people bought tickets well in advance, because every game was a sell-out, and they had hundreds of entrances to filter the fans through safely. You wouldn't fancy causing any bother, either, with armed police and militia buzzing all over the place. Barcelona, and many of the other top Spanish clubs, had efficient membership schemes long before they were envisaged in Britain and for many of the matches you have to be a registered supporter to even get a sniff of a ticket. Coaches are laid on from both the city centre and the provinces to get people into the grounds safely.

On one occasion while I was out there Bobby Charlton and Alex Ferguson came to our matches to see how it was achieved as there was no equivalent anywhere in Britain. Even inside the ground, the Spanish have a way of doing things that makes football a pleasure to watch. The stands were seven or eight tiers high, with huge walkways between the rows, and vendors would stroll around the ground selling wine and sandwiches. When I first saw this, at the training ground for Terry's welcoming speech, I thought it was something that had been laid on just for that day. But every match was highly organized in the same way: wine, sandwiches, hot dogs, special beefburger steaks and more ice cold beer. It made a football match a real night out.

When the teams came out there was a hail of firecrackers and confetti and bands would play. It was such a big occasion, and yet so relaxed. Fans didn't care if matches kicked-off ten or fifteen minutes late, they waited patiently, soaking up the atmosphere. It was rare to see any trouble on the terraces behind the goals, but if there was, the police had no hesitation sending in the dogs. Everything about the club was professional and expertly planned.

It was Terry's duty, once a week, to lunch with the chairman, president and the boys from the Barcelona Academy – twenty or thirty highly-talented youngsters, the pick of the crop from the local area and beyond. Some, like Nayim, who

Terry brought with him to Tottenham, came from as far away as Morocco to work with the acedemy's coaches. It was a brilliantly-run training school, on similar lines to the FA's own School of Excellence at Lilleshall, yet it actually belonged to one club. They were educated by their own teachers, and given football coaching under the same roof. The academy had its own kitchens, sleeping quarters – everthing a boy could possibly need.

When the first team trained in the morning the academy's pupils would often come to watch and learn, standing behind a sixteen-foot high wire mesh fence. You think of Tottenham or Manchester United being a big club until you see that. Next to the academy was Barcelona's own skating rink, which could accommodate 1,500 kids at one time, and their top-of-the league basketball stadium where you'd see seven-foot Spaniards, Moroccans, blacks and whites training every day. They were the European Cup winners and so successful they even imported talent from America. Nearby was the 60,000 capacity training ground and athletics club.

The team coach had telephones for the players, television and video – it was top of the range. But the club preferred to fly to a lot of their matches. Clubs like Majorca could only be approached by plane and other places such as Bilbao were too far away, so they would hop on a plane and be there in an hour. I used to sit with Terry and he'd say to me: 'This is the way to go to watch football, Fred.' Well, it certainly beats a ten-mile tailback on the M1!

Even the Press was different in Barcelona. They had the regular daily papers with their normal quota of sports pages plus three – *Sport, Dicen* and *El Mundo Deportivo* – with the contents devoted to sport alone. Barcelona FC was their main interest, and every day they had to come up with twelve pages of news on the club, which is how the manager's dad found himself pictured on page one! It meant that stories were often exaggerated because of the need to fill so many pages, but Terry was prepared for that before he arrived. He held a Press conference almost every day after training, and after matches there would always be twenty or thirty reporters, plus television and radio men waiting to be seen.

Often the reporters would just send young boys down with cassette machines to record the interview. Then they would run like errand boys back to the top journalists, who would put Terry's words in the paper. Their other trick was to employ attractive, female reporters to get their stories, and sometimes the constant attention from all sides must have frustrated Terry. But it was hard to fall out with the editor of the *Sport* paper. He was a smashing man, and every Thursday we would all go out to lunch, to lovely restaurants, a different venue almost every time, and we'd have a meal and a chat. He couldn't do enough for you, and as Terry's father I was made to feel a real celebrity. There was never any snobbery at Barcelona, everyone made you feel welcome and important. 'I'm nearly famous,' I'd joke with Terry, but he always remained level-headed about the attention. 'I've got to succeed in Barcelona, dad,' he would say, 'or they won't want to know me. If you're a failure out here, every-thing changes.'

I know it was difficult for him at first. The new season began with everyone questioning the summer transfer of Maradona, and the arrival of the unknown Steve Archibald. The Barcelona board wanted Mexican striker Hugo Sanchez, but Terry stuck to his guns and insisted on Steve – he knew he had to win his first battle with them. The Press christened Steve 'Archi-goles' but they still seemed to have many more doubts than Terry. It was a hard time and although everyone was friendly, I think it still did Terry good to see a face from home.

In his first season I went out there for a few days and

finished up staying six weeks! Every time I announced I was going to fly back, Terry would say: 'Well, we've got a good game next week,' and I'd stay on just a little while longer. Luckily, Terry's new career in Barcelona got off to a flying start. They won a four-club tournament held at the Nou Camp stadium, beating Argentina side Boca Juniors 9–1, and the famous West Germans Bayern Munich 3–1. Archibald scored twice against Boca, and the atmosphere in the city seemed to change almost immediately. Wherever Terry went people would come up to his car and bang on the windscreen, cheering his name. It helped that there was no real rival to Barcelona in the town, and the majority of people seemed united for a common cause.

They desperately wanted to beat old enemies Real Madrid, in the first League game of the season, and tickets for that match were already changing hands on the black market for £125. Terry could have fallen flat on his face that day, had Madrid won comfortably, instead Barcelona got off to a cracking start, winning away at the home of their rivals. In all his time out there, Terry only lost one of thirteen games against Real Madrid, and his record in his first season with Barcelona was magnificent. They were nine points clear of Atletico Madrid with twelve matches to go, and had the title sewn up by the end of March. It was a fantastic achievement for a manager in his first season and not bad considering the pressure he was under to succeed. He even signed a contract, at the directors' request, saying the decision to buy Archibald was his alone. They wanted to make sure Terry would take the blame if the move didn't work out – that's how much faith they had in him. He was happy to sign and was proved right, and as soon as I heard news of the title win I flew out there in time to see Terry and his side play their first game at Nou Camp as Champions, against Sporting Gijon.

The fans made such a fuss that the match kicked off twenty-five minutes late. There were the usual firecrackers and confetti, plus so many flags you couldn't believe there was a spare piece of cloth left intact in the city. And drums! I thought the ringing in my ears would never stop after the ovation the players received. The pitch was swarming with dancers and celebrities, and at one time I thought they were all going to forget about the match and just have the party instead! But Barcelona beat Gijon 2–0 to cap one of the proudest nights of Papa Venables's life.

8

Terry bought his own apartment in Barcelona, quite near the Nou Camp stadium, on a long avenue that eventually made its way out to the Cadiz Road. Whenever I went out there that is where I stayed, and it really was the most glamorous place. Terry's apartment ran the length of the building, with a long corridor and bedrooms and bathrooms leading off. It had an outdoor swimming pool, and I had my own bedroom with a veranda and a spectacular view of the town. It couldn't have been more different from the two-bedroomed council house in Bonham Road, Dagenham, and took my breath away the first time I stepped inside. There was a garage under the block, and as Terry came along the road in his Porsche, he could press a button on the remote control and the doors would open allowing him to swing straight in. He had a key to his own lift, which would travel up and then stop inside his own apartment – the flats were very secure and that was the only entrance.

We had some laughs up in that flat. One day, I had been out for a few drinks with Terry, and we'd come back very much the worse for wear. I was staggering around the flat, moaning and groaning because I couldn't find the tea, then I collapsed in a chair and fell asleep. What I didn't know was that while I was snoring, Toots (Terry's girlfriend after his amicable split with Christine), had closed the curtains, turned all the lights out in the room and put heavy black masking tape over the lenses of my glasses. I woke up to one of the most frightening experiences of my life. The room was in total darkness and I felt very disorientated. I was fumbling about and eventually found my glasses but I still couldn't make anything out. I started calling out: 'Help me, I've gone blind!' Terry ran into the room, feigning concern, and switched all the lights on, but of course it made no difference. Now I was really in a state. 'I can't see, I can't see,' I kept shouting. Finally, he reached over, pulled my glasses off and I was flooded by light. 'What are you talking about, you soppy old sod?' he said.

Toots was always playing tricks like that. Once, after a visit, I returned to Heathrow Airport to find a customs official looking very suspiciously at my passport. 'Is this your picture, sir?' he asked. 'Of course it is,' I replied, only to look down and see that she had stuck a photograph of Idi Amin where my picture should have been! That time, the official smiled and laughed it off, but the chap we had running our pub in Epping wasn't so lucky. Toots pulled the same stunt on him, but he obviously got one of the humourless officials at the airport because they took him into a sideroom and detained him for two hours! He had the hump about that for weeks afterwards.

However, the joke was on Terry the day his daughter, Nancy, and Toots brought Bilko the puppy home from the pet shop. Nancy is dog mad and she had been pestering Terry for a puppy for ages, but he had always refused. One day he was lying on the settee when the door opened and in came Nancy with the most beautiful little pup you've ever seen. It was white and fluffy with a brown patch over one eye – anyone would have fallen in love with it. But Terry was in a real flap. 'What in hell's name is that?' he cried. 'It's only little,' said Nancy, plonking it down on his glass-topped table, 'and I've spoken to the lady in the shop and she said it's not going to grow any bigger.' Terry couldn't believe what he was seeing. It was a tiny thing, sure, but it had the biggest paws of any dog he'd seen – like dustbin lids as he clambered all over the apartment. 'Are you sure,' he said, 'are you sure it won't get any bigger? It looks to me like it's going to be a big dog.' Terry was proved right. Harmless little Bilko grew up to be a bloody great Pyrenean Mountain dog, the aristocratic relative of the St Bernard. There's a marvellous photograph of Bilko, standing on two legs next to Terry on his balcony, and he's a good two inches taller. Terry put his arm around the dog, and Bilko put his front paw around Terry – it's one of the most comical things I've seen. Terry used to joke he would sell the car, buy a saddle and ride Bilko into work instead.

It was useless having a dog that size in Terry's apartment. He produced more mess than any dog I've ever seen, for a start, and he could be a vicious so-and-so. I came out of the lift with Bilko one day, and he bit a woman who was waiting patiently at the bottom to go up. Terry got fined for that. Bilko's problem was that he needed room, he hated being cooped up in the flat all day, he'd bark and cry and howl whenever you went out. But whenever we tried to take him for walks ourselves it was a nightmare. We'd get out into the street, Bilko would know where he was going, I wouldn't and he'd pull me arse over tip!

Terry was the same, we'd see them coming down the street and Terry would have a worried look on his face, tip-toeing along like he was on feathers. Because if Bilko saw another dog he'd be after it, and it was as much as you could do to stop him yanking your arm out of its socket. Terry would wrap his leather lead two or three times around trees to stop him running away, but it did no good. Once Bilko snapped the lead completely in half – he had the strength of ten men. Bilko hardly added to the friendly atmosphere in Terry's posh apartment block. When Terry moved in everyone loved him as the manager of Barcelona. Once Bilko arrived it was as much as he could do to get his neighbours to say 'hello'.

We had to take the pressure off in some way, and a friend of ours, a waiter called Paco offered to take Bilko for a month because his mate, Manolo, insisted. Paco was a little man and he had to be to get inside his flat which was no bigger than a telephone box. Bilko had to be reversed out of Paco's place every morning as there was no room for him to turn – he was touching all four walls! Paco was determined not to let the dog affect his social life, and he took Bilko with him everywhere. He was a great night-club man, and he'd turn up at these exclusive places and the little flap in the door would open, and there would be Paco. 'It's OK, come in,' the doorman would say, and in bounded Bilko, tearing around the disco and knocking the dancers over. Terry saw the pair of them one night, out on the town. Paco was creeping the night away on the dancefloor with a pretty girl, Bilko was in the corner with a big pint of lager, slurping away and surrounded by people fussing over him and saying 'what a lovely dog'.

It was a sad day, but Bilko had to go, and the waiter at the Princess Sophia Hotel took him to his little farm up in the hills, where he lives to this day with sixteen other dogs. I'm sure he's happier now than he ever could have been in that apartment, and every time Terry returns to Barcelona, he catches up on the latest stories – Bilko hasn't changed!

Things were always happening to Terry in Barcelona. He hadn't been there long when he discovered just how strongly the people of Barcelona had taken to him. He was driving home late one night when a motorcyclist smashed into his car at high speed. The poor bloke was taken to hospital with a broken leg, and Terry looked as if he could be in trouble with the police. The next day Terry visited the chap in hospital, and every paper in Barcelona carried pictures of them on the front page smiling and shaking hands. The motorcyclist's name was Jorge Alvarez-Giral and he turned out to be a big fan of Barcelona. Terry returned to the hospital with a football signed by the entire team and Jorge was delighted. There were more handshakes and smiles and as Terry was about to leave he apologized again for the accident. 'Oh don't say sorry,' said Jorge, cheerfully. 'You have made me famous, Meester Ben-a-bless!' It was something that couldn't have happened anywhere but Barcelona, and reflected how strongly the people felt abut Terry bringing the Championship to their city.

If anything, Terry's next season was even more spectacular and he came within moments of becoming a legend in Spain for bringing Barcelona their first European Cup title. The season began in a most incredible fashion with an incident that showed just how fierce the spotlight was on Barcelona. Steve Archibald returned for pre-season training wearing a diamond-studded earring of the kind that was fashionable in Britain at the time. At Spurs it would hardly have warranted a mention, but at Barcelona? All hell was let loose! Steve's ear-hole was given the full close-up treatment in the newspapers, and everyone seemed to be walking around in a state of shock.

Terry had to take Steve to one side and tell him: 'This is the land of the matadors. They are not used to their sportsmen wearing earrings. I don't care what you do in your own life, but it's probably best you don't wear it to the training ground again.' But Steve, like Terry as a young man, was always ready with his own question. 'Why?' he asked. 'Because it's not worth the trouble,' Terry told him. 'But other players wear jewellery, like necklaces and rings, why should anyone think different of me over this?' Terry gave it more thought. 'Steve,' he said, 'what would you say to a bloke who turned up for training in a tiara – that's jewellery!'

With the argument won and stability restored, Barcelona could now begin their assault on the European Cup, and they had a close shave in the first leg, winning on the away goals rule after a 2–2 aggregate draw with Czechoslovakian side Sparta Prague. Steve Archibald scored a vital goal at Porto to send them through on away goals again, this time following a 3–3 draw, and then it was on to the tie of the tournament – the quarter-finals against Juventus. Barcelona won 1–0 at home, and the 1–1 draw they got in Turin, with another goal from Archibald, must count as one of Terry's managerial triumphs.

Juventus, European Cup-winners in the previous season, were hot favourites to win the tournament and Barcelona's slender lead was thought to be nowhere near strong enough to give them a chance against the Italians. Even Terry conceded it was the greatest performance of any team he had managed to get a draw out there, and he now stood just two matches away from a European Final.

It was ironic, in many ways, that having got to the final on penalties, Barcelona should then lose in Seville the same heart-breaking way – but that is what happened. Having lost the first-leg of the semi 3–0 in Gothenburg no-one gave Terry's side a prayer in the rematch, but a hat-trick from

Picho Alonso took the game into a penalty shoot-out, and Barcelona won 5–4. I was jumping for joy when I heard. I've seen Terry win Championships, FA Cups and play for his country on many occasions at different levels, but what could compare to a European Cup Final?

Terry was under no illusions about what it could mean to him. 'It's something they've never been near winning,' he told me. 'Bringing that to Barcelona is as near as you can get to becoming a legend out here.'

Unfortunately, I couldn't get out to see the Final in Seville on 7 May 1986, but once again the television cameras were in the pub, soaking up the atmosphere while everyone soaked up the free beer. I've always thought games as big as that should not be decided on penalties, and it was a soul-destroying feeling to see Steaua Bucharest's goalkeeper Helmut Ducadam dive to his left to save the fourth Barcelona penalty from Marcos. Terry phoned me that night, and he couldn't believe it either. 'We had it there for the taking,' he kept saying, and I could sense the terrible disappointment in his voice. To be so close to something only to have it taken away from you like that must be the worst feeling in the world, and the team he had built at Barcelona was so strong as well.

I have never claimed to be a football expert, but I've spent a lot of my time watching the game, first when Terry was a player, then later watching the teams he produced as a manager, and I'd say I've never seen a better striker of the ball than Bernd Schuster, the West German international at Barcelona. After training, the players would go for a bath or a rub-down, but Schuster would often stay behind for extra practice and I'd watch him, mesmerized. He could make the ball do anything, and he'd stand out almost by the corner flag curling it into the net at an incredible angle. He would work with one of the younger lads or a goalkeeper and he would do it for what seemed like hours – one after the other, bang, bang, bang into the net. He was a magnificent footballer, but seemed a very weak man, completely in the control of his wife. She seemed to act as his agent, and whatever she said went.

It was interesting to watch the different personalities come together at Barcelona as a team. Steve Archibald settled in well from the start, and I never found him unfriendly as his reputation in Britain would suggest. He had his own friends out there and played snooker and tennis but whenever I saw him at the Princess Sofia Hotel or one of the restaurants, he would always stop and come over for a drink.

The most amusing thing was to watch the Spanish players train. They had a regular routine. Terry would go into the office at nine o'clock to open his mail, while Allan Harris warmed up the team. Terry would then get on to the training field about half-an-hour later. The first time I watched them the temperature must have been pushing seventy degrees, yet all of the players were wearing tracksuit bottoms. Terry, Allan, and Terry's bodyguard Jose (who trained with the team to help work off some of his fat) were the only ones in shorts, and I was standing on the touchline waiting for everybody to get stripped and ready for action. But that was how the players endured the entire two-hour session in searing heat. I couldn't work it out. One of the players was even wearing gloves, and I couldn't resist asking Terry what was going on. 'They always train like that,' he said, quite matter-of-factly, 'because they feel the cold.' 'But it's a blazing hot day,' I protested, in my shirt-sleeves. 'Not to them, it's not,' he replied, 'they're freezing.' The whole situation left me astonished. If they think Barcelona's cold, they should try working down the docks on a Thursday morning in February – that would sort them out!

The 'cold' weather didn't stop Barcelona's players training, I've never seen a team prepared to work so hard. There was no sloppiness, and no half-measures in the practice matches, either. It wasn't unusual to see four or five players receiving treatment after a particularly rough session, and it sometimes surprised me that we had a team left to field on match days!

All of the players were prepared to work at their fitness, and I think they enjoyed the new ideas Terry brought to the club. He got them working as a team, and not as individuals. I think it comes down to the spirit of the matador that I mentioned before. Spanish footballers demand to be recognized as individual talents, and are not so interested in teamwork. Terry changed that, and once the players saw it produced winning football, Championship trophies and other medals, they were more than willing to accept his methods.

When Barcelona were really buzzing, they looked ten times faster than almost any team I've ever seen. I think for the first few weeks the players were very sombre when Terry was about, they didn't know quite what he was going to do. But once he had brought them the Championship and European success the atmosphere lightened considerably, and they began laughing and joking with the rest. They were always very friendly when I was around. I could go into the dressing-room and they would try to have a conversation with me in a pidgin English, it was very nice.

Terry's next plan was to add yet more Englishmen to Barcelona's exclusive club of Anglo exiles – three million pounds worth of talent in the shape of strikers Gary Lineker, from Everton, and Mark Hughes of Manchester United. When Terry had bought Steve Archibald in his first weeks at the club one of his main priorities was to make sure Steve would be the sort of person who would settle-in quickly on the Continent. He knew he had only a short space of time to prove himself, and he wanted a player who could acclimatize quickly to football and life abroad.

He singled out Mark and Gary for the same reasons, but

unfortunately with Mark it was not to be. He would come in and train every day, and was totally committed to the club, but I'm not sure Mark could ever throw himself in the same way into mastering the language. I could understand his thinking, because players can often only be abroad for a couple of years, and he did his best. I think to get the most out of a move like that you have to be able to do a bit more than muddle through. It's only a small point, and I'm sure it wouldn't have made the slightest difference had things been working for him on the field, but Mark and Gary could never seem to strike up the right partnership together.

They didn't work well as a striking combination, Mark couldn't score and he wasn't getting the right balls through for Gary to make the same impact, either. And Mark had a problem with Spanish referees. So much of his game relies on the physical approach, and they weren't used to seeing a forward who gave the hatchetman as good as he got. They were on his back almost from the start, and a lot of his power was lost by cutting out that part of his game. He was penalised so much he must have felt like tearing his hair out. It was a shame because when I watched Mark in training he looked a brilliant player, but had one of those runs where nothing seemed to go right for him. I'm sure all good players have known the feeling at one time or another in their careers. It might have been the environment, it could be any one of a number of reasons, but Mark was getting criticized by the fans in every game, and Terry knew something had to be done about it.

Spain has a completely different set-up to England, and it was one of the toughest decisions Terry has had to make to drop Mark Hughes from the first-team pool. In Spain, clubs have to register a squad of players, and their team has to be picked from that group. There is no question of drafting men in from the reserves and it was Terry's decision to change his pool half-way through the season, bringing Steve Archibald back in for Hughes. In many ways, I think it came as almost a relief for Mark. He knew he hadn't been playing well, and it was probably doing his confidence no good to be in the fans' firing line all the time. Terry would remember that feeling himself from Tottenham, and in Terry's position sometimes you have to be ruthless.

I can remember a time when a manager running one of our pubs had been doing a bad job and we wanted to give him the sack. I couldn't bring myself to do it, but Terry said: 'In my job, once a year I have to look at a bunch of kids who have done nothing wrong at all, good kids who have behaved themselves all year, and tell them they are leaving the club because I don't think they are good enough. For a lot of them it's the end of all their hopes and dreams, and I'm the man who has to do it. If I'm capable of that, I'm capable of this. If you want the manager sacked, I'll tell him.'

It was with that same approach that he told Mark Hughes he was out of the first-team squad. It's not a nice job, but someone has to do it. The same would have been true of Gary Lineker. Now that Terry is his manager again at Spurs people talk of their 'special relationship' and it goes without saying that they get on well with each other, and each has a strong admiration for the ability of the other. But, believe me, if there was ever a time when Terry felt Gary could no longer perform at the highest level, he would have no hesitation in dropping him. You cannot have favourites in football, the rest of the team would suss you out too quickly and it could also cost you your job as a manager or coach.

Terry's rapport with Gary came from one reason only – he did an excellent job for him at Barcelona. Gary wholeheartedly threw himself into life at Barcelona, both on and off the field. He took regular lessons, as Terry had, to master the language, and quickly adapted to the way the team played.

Fred with his wife, Myrtle, on their wedding day, 21 November 1941

Myrtle, Fred and Terry, 1946. This will always be Terry's favourite photograph.

ABOVE *Terry on holiday in Margate, circa 1949*

RIGHT *Terry, Myrtle and Fred dancing at Warners Holiday Camp, 1950*

Myrtle with Terry at the social club in Rainham, 1950

Terry and friends at the Winding Way Social Club

BELOW *School trip for Terry and his chums to Portsmouth. Terry returned as top sailor, 1956*

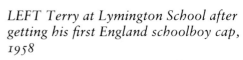

LEFT Terry at Lymington School after getting his first England schoolboy cap, 1958

BELOW LEFT Terry and Fred in their garden in Bonham Road, Dagenham, Terry wearing his first England schoolboy shirt, 1958

BELOW Running out with the first team at Chelsea, aged seventeen

Terry in Dagenham schoolboy team, 1958

RIGHT Terry singing at the Hammersmith Palais with the Joe Loss band, 1959

Chelsea Youth Team in Cannes, 1959. Terry is second from left, front row

Terry on holiday in Greece with Chelsea Youth team, 1958

Chelsea Youth Team sightseeing in Greece, 1958

Terry and some of the Chelsea Youth Team at Butlins, Clacton, 1960. They returned with a few trophies

On the beach, Chris, Terry and Myrtle take the sun at Margate, 1970

Chelsea v Burnley, 1960. Terry's first away match for the first team, aged seventeen

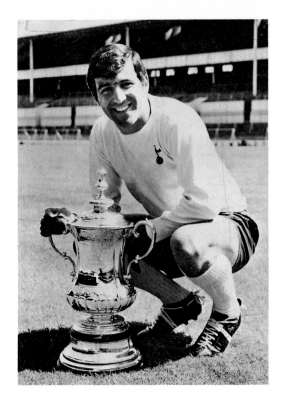

Terry with the FA Cup which Spurs won in 1967

Terry playing for QPR in 1970

Terry in Spurs FA Cup winning team, 1967

Manager of the Year after winning the Spanish League, holding the trophy – the first time Barcelona had won it in sixteen years. What an achievement for the boy from Dagenham, 1984

Fred with Barcelona player Steve Archibald, 1984

Fred outside a fish shop in Barcelona, 1984

ABOVE RIGHT The artist and gallery owner, John Marti, with Terry, and the completed portrait which now hangs in Terry's house, 1985

BELOW RIGHT Gary Lineker, his wife, Michelle, and her sister, at the Capri Beach Club, Barcelona, owned by a friend of Terry's

Fred pictured with the speedboat sponsored by father and son

The winning speedboat – adorned with cups – 1988

Fred and Terry at the Royal Oak enjoying a little Christmas spirit, 1989

The Royal Oak, Sewardstone Road, Chingford, which Fred Venables took over as a free house in 1980

Terry's daughters at Nancy's wedding, Nancy on the left, Tracey on the right, 8 July 1989

Myrtle and Fred enjoying the evening's celebrations at the Royal Lancaster after Nancy's wedding

Terry in a pensive mood, talking to the Press at Spurs football ground, 1988

Terry Venables, 'Gazza' and Paul Stewart promote Spurs video, 1989

FOLLOWING PAGE Terry coaching in Barcelona before the European Cup match with Juventus

He, and his wife Michelle, obviously loved the way of life over there, and I have always believed a settled home environment can only help a player when he comes out to do his job on a Saturday.

I have always liked to think that Terry's upbringing in our little Bonham Road mid-terrace contributed in a positive way to his early matches with Chelsea. Similarly, when you saw Gary and Michelle with friends in a restaurant or at a club you got the feeling he would be going into matches with no real outside pressures. I liked both Gary and Mark, but you could sense one was far happier in Barcelona than the other.

For my part, I've never known a city so friendly or a club that gave you so many opportunities to really experience the good life. On my living room walls at the pub in Chingford I've got paintings and tapestries presented to me by Spanish people when I visited Terry. He made friends with one of the top artists in Spain, and I've got one of his paintings hanging in the pub. When Terry flew down to guest on a television show in Madrid, they presented him with an original by the surrealist Salvador Dali.

Wherever Barcelona went they travelled in style, and I visited some fantastic places on their trips around Europe. I can remember a trip to Milan and visiting a magnificent hotel on the edge of Lake Como that had been a setting for one of the James Bond films only a few months earlier. We took a boat trip around the lake before mooring up outside the hotel and four of us – Terry, Allan Harris, Terry's friend and business partner Paul Kirby, and myself, had lunch on the patio. It started to rain and the waiter came out and set up four individual umbrellas to keep us dry. It really was the most picturesque surrounding.

Paul runs a development company in the City of London and he was always flying over to meet up with Terry on his trips abroad. When Barcelona played Dundee United in the

UEFA Cup, the teams stayed at the famous Old Course Golf and Country Club in St Andrews and Paul was due to fly in to Edinburgh that day. But he went one better. We were sitting in the lounge when there was this almighty clattering of engines and a helicopter came down on the landing pad just outside in the gardens. Paul stepped out and asked the pilot to wait, and then he took us all for a flight over the dunes and local scenery. It was the first time I'd ever been in a helicopter and the feeling was quite exhilarating, a great thrill. Even at my age there are some things that can make you feel like a kid again.

But all good things have to come to an end, and towards the close of Terry's third season, there were rumblings that things weren't going right. Barcelona were still runners-up in the League, but after winning the Championship in his first season the fans had high expectations. You can overstay your welcome at any club and three full seasons at Barcelona is longer than I think anyone felt Terry would last. He'd spent three Christmases in Spain (one of Barcelona's coaches had predicted he wouldn't make it past his first), he'd won the League for the first time in twenty years, and only a penalty shoot-out stood between Barcelona and their first European Cup trophy – it's a record many managers would kill for.

In the end, the politics of Barcelona dictated that Terry had to move on. When crowds of 120,000 start dropping to 70,000 they get worried, and Terry knew he would have to leave sooner or later. He never had any real problems with the supporters, even at the end, although I suppose you could say that was natural when policemen are patrolling the ground with dogs and sticks a yard long wrapped around their hands with leather straps.

The bottom line is that Barcelona have eighteen directors who could easily be sacked, or voted out just like the manager. In the end, Terry's departure saved their jobs.

I've got a lot of happy memories of Barcelona, and it wasn't easy for Terry whatever certain people say. When he was out there I think he got sick of reading stories about John Toshack, at Real Sociedad, telling everybody how much money Barcelona had to spend, and how he was struggling because Sociedad could only sign players from the Basque region. For a start, the Basque country is bigger than England, and I don't think anyone would take seriously a complaint that went 'Oh, I've only got England to choose from'. Secondly, with all their restrictions, Sociedad had still experienced more success in the last two decades than Barcelona. Terry's Championship win was their first in almost two decades – Sociedad and Bilbao had both won it more than once. With Madrid so against them it is difficult for Barcelona to achieve anything in Spanish football, and I think that is where Terry proved his ability as a manager once and for all. Forget what others might say about the money he had to spend at Nou Camp. Previous Barcelona managers had had the same advantages and still couldn't bring success. Maradona came and went without the title arriving, and Johann Cruyff has not managed it since taking over from Terry. No, mark my words, Terry won the League at Barcelona because he did a damn good job.

9

*T*erry's first meeting with the man who was to become his co-writer of the Hazell books came when he was just nineteen. Gordon Williams was employed as a ghost writer for Chelsea's manager, Tommy Docherty, and travelled regularly to the Naafi ground at Mitcham, where the club trained. Terry had recently been made captain, and it was Docherty who introduced him to Gordon. I don't think the meeting was a remarkable one. Terry always claims never to have read a book at school, and back then I don't think he had anything on his mind except football. Gordon lived around the Shepherd's Bush area, and was a regular at Stamford Bridge, and over the years the pair stayed in touch. Gordon worked on a variety of local newspapers and magazines, and had written novels of his own. But, in 1967, he was compiling the brochure for the FA Cup Final between Spurs and Chelsea, and it brought him into contact with Terry again. Gordon's job was to write a brief profile of every player, in their own words, but Terry decided to write his own. He was the only player to do so, and by then had caught the writing bug badly.

In those days if a footballer supplied his name to a magazine article, the fee was split down the middle between the subject of the piece and the ghost writer. Terry decided to cut out the middle man and did the lot himself. His first article was called 'Jokes the Fans Don't Hear' and appeared virtually word for word.

Now he wanted to do more, and like many of the best ideas, the decision to write a novel with Gordon came out of a casual conversation. Terry had an idea to write a book about football, drawing on his own experiences and those of other players. He knew what he wanted to say, but was unsure of how to go about it. Gordon, whose own novels included *Straw Dogs*, knew how to put the words on paper, and together they began to write a book entitled *They Used to Play on Grass*. Terry had always written short stories for his own amusement, but this was the first time he had tried anything with a view to publication. Terry and Gordon used a small office in London and every day after training Terry would drive there to work on the book. He was so determined to do it, I knew he would succeed.

Terry has always been like that, throughout his life, and once he said to me he was working on a book I knew he would not let up until he was satisfied. Terry and Gordon would be up there for hours, no half measures, and by that time Terry had even learned to type. Almost every story and anecdote in the book was true, so the pair had to disguise the sources and characters. That was why they set the book in the future, at a big London club, with a boardroom power struggle going on behind the scenes.

Reading the book now, it is amazing to see how accurate

some of their predictions have been. There's the title for a start – *They Used to Play on Grass* – well, we all know who put a stop to that! In Terry's book, the FA Cup had been replaced by the British Cup, and teams from England could be drawn away to Rangers or Celtic in Scotland. It's interesting how many times that has been suggested since. One of my favourite stories from the book is completely true and concerns a manager who also had a passion for greyhounds. When the players came in for treatment on Mondays they would be unable to get on the table, because the manager would have his dog in for rehabilitation instead! Finally, one of the players had enough, and suggested to the manager: 'I think he's putting it on to miss training, boss!' I know Terry was disappointed at people's reactions when the book was published. A few newspapers produced their review on the sports pages, not the books page, and seemed unwilling to take it seriously. A lot of people suggested Terry's involvement was a gimmick and that he had contributed little himself. Some would ask if Terry had done any of the actual writing, when in fact, two of the best-received passages were constructed by Terry alone. I think there is still a lot of snobbery from people outside and inside football, and they get the idea that the players are morons, unable to string two words together in a coherent sentence. They couldn't get used to the fact that a footballer could go out on to the field on Saturday, and write books in his spare time. Terry and Gordon were determined to have another go to prove the critics wrong, and this time they would use a pseudonym.

Ernie Yuill was a close friend of the family when Terry was very small. He used to work with me in the docks and lived nearby in Dagenham. We'd always knock around together and Ernie would come to all of Terry's matches for Dagenham schools and the district. He and his wife Mary would sometimes look after Terry while Myrtle and I were out at work, and he was a mad keen football fan. He supported Millwall, who were only a Third Division club at the time, but he encouraged Terry in all walks of life. So when Terry decided to write under an assumed name, he picked out P. B. Yuill as a tribute to Ernie.

The original plan for the book was for Gordon and Terry to write a weepie, in the style of *Love Story*. It was the hit film of that year, and Terry got the idea when he went to see his new-born baby daughter Nancy in hospital. She was in a large room with tens of other babies, and had a tiny identity-tag bound around her wrist, but it had come loose and was almost falling off. It set Terry thinking: what if the name-tags were mixed up ... what if two mothers left hospital with the wrong babies ... That was the basis for Gordon and Terry's next book, but the problem was they couldn't take it seriously.

Gordon is a hard-bitten cynical Scotsman and add that to Terry's upbringing in east London, and you had two men who could never write a sob story without laughing. They had written ten heart-wrenching chapters, but every time they should have been wringing their hankies out they were collapsing into giggles. By that stage in the story they had one of the American mothers involved in a car crash and needing a blood transfusion to save her baby's life. But no blood will match and, realizing what has happened, she becomes desperate to swop the babies back. Terry admits that by this time he was laughing himself silly, so he tossed the manuscript in the drawer and thought: forget it. This is when the private eye James Hazell entered the scene.

Gordon and Terry wanted a man who could look at life with their own slightly cynical eye. They decided the only way they could continue writing the book would be to put a street-smart private eye on the case – James Hazell. Again, the name was taken from Terry's past, from a chap he used to play football with. Jimmy Hazell was a centre-half from Terry's younger days, not a particularly close friend, but a name that has always stuck in Terry's mind. The physical description of James Hazell in the books came from someone completely different – England's captain of the day, Bobby Moore. Terry threw in a bit of himself, a bit of Bobby and a bit of Billy Walker to create the private detective Hazell – he didn't want to write him as a James Bond-style superhero, but a normal bloke, with normal problems who has a smile at life. Terry said: 'He's like the weather forecast – bright in patches.'

Inventing Hazell gave Terry and Gordon a new problem because they had to keep coming up with funny, sharp lines for a variety of situations. Hazell had to be able to walk into a launderette to get his washing done and make it funny, and worrying about getting the jokes right used to keep Terry awake at night. You'd hear Gordon and Terry ringing each other for advice on what Hazell would say in certain situations, and in their office on Oxford Street in central London, they'd swop notes and jokes until they came up with the right combination. A lot of Terry's friends got a namecheck in the book. Tom Griffiths, the haulage contractor from Terry's childhood, became the Mr Big of bookmaking in the book. 'He had a wad big enough to choke a spin-dryer,' is one of Terry's favourite lines. The book was published under the title *Hazell Plays Solomon,* written by one P.B. Yuill. It was only when Macmillan, the publishers, asked them for a follow-up that Gordon and Terry revealed their true identity – but by then there were even bigger plans afoot.

Hazell was turned into a television series, and the auditions for the lead role took place at my pub in Chingford. Terry's original choice for the part would have been John Bindon, but it went to a then unknown young actor called Nicholas Ball.

We had the cameras set up in my lounge near the bar, and Terry drove over to give his views on the casting. It will go down as one of the proudest moments of my life. I suppose there was a certain stage in Terry's career when I expected him to become a success at football. Once your boy had played for England at every level and captained Chelsea at such a young age you can predict that there will be moments of great personal achievement. But to see him as the author of books and the writer of a television series was something else. This from the boy teachers always complained would never concentrate on his lessons, and from a boy whose claim was to never have read a book in his schooldays. It was quite remarkable. The series was later sold to Australian television, and when Terry joined Barcelona as manager, the Hazell books suddenly appeared all over the city translated into Spanish. It really took off over there.

I'm sure there must have been times since when Terry has considered a full-time career as a writer. But that was just one of his many options – he can sing as well.

Terry has never felt uncomfortable with a lot of the glamour and publicity that surrounds football, and I'm sure I know the reason behind that. Deep down, he has always loved to be on a stage. I don't mean that in a big-headed way, because he has never been one to blow his own trumpet. From a very early age, he has enjoyed getting up in front of people and performing, and as a boy he would always be singing or miming to records.

In fact, when he was only four he joined a little song and dance troupe called the Happy Tappers. He was one of the youngest kids there, in his little velvet top hat, suit and bow tie, and his tiny tap-dancing shoes. His nan, Millie, would get him dressed up in the gear and they would go round to St Thomas's church hall in Hayden Road, Dagenham (Myrtle and I were married there). They would put on shows for anyone who would watch, and the sixpence admission money went to charity. Terry could tap and sing, and I can still remember some of their routines – 'Don't Fence Me in', 'On the Sunny Side of the Street' and 'An Apple Blossom Wedding'. We'd take him to a lot of the local clubs and pubs after school to sing and mime. There was one, the Winding Way Club, which we nicknamed 'the slippery slidey club', because the kids were always falling over on the heavily-polished floors and stage. We'd also go to the pub around the corner from our house in Bonham Road, the Hind's Head. Terry would mime to records by Spike Jones and his City Slickers and Jimmy Durante, and it was comical to hear the Schnoz's unmistakable voice seemingly coming out of the mouth of one so small.

I think that is where Terry caught the showbiz bug, and as a teenager the posters of Dave Mackay and Danny Blanchflower on his wall hung side by side with ones of Buddy Holly and Elvis Presley. Dagenham produced a few pop stars of its own, and as an apprentice at Chelsea, Terry would regularly travel up to London with a lad called Brian Poole, who became the lead singer of The Tremeloes.

Not that Terry's singing career impressed everybody. He was often in trouble with Tommy Docherty at Chelsea for entering local talent contests. He would dodge Tommy to go out and try his luck in the shows, organized by Butlin's Holidays. Terry won all his heats, but Tommy caught up with him and banned him from entering the final. The Bachelors went on to win it, so you never know what might have happened had Terry competed.

When Terry sung with Joe Loss at the Hammersmith Palais, Docherty dropped him on the Saturday, and one nightclub even offered him one hundred pounds a week to front their band. When Terry asked Docherty's permission he was told to choose between football or a stage career, he couldn't have both – playing for Chelsea won.

But not completely. Terry now turned his attention to writing his own songs, and every day after training he'd go up to Denmark Street in London, Tin Pan Alley as it was known, and he would try to write songs, hanging around with the professionals who frequented the 142 Club. The players had a regular routine at Chelsea. They would finish training at twelve-thirty, by the time they had a shower it would be one o'clock and the lads would then go to a local snooker hall for their dinner. They'd have a few games in the afternoon, maybe a couple of drinks and then it would be time for tea. A lot of the players never saw daylight once they had stepped off the training field at the end of a morning session; not Terry.

He had to find something else to keep his mind active, and he would go straight up town after training to begin work on his songwriting sideline. He became great pals with a very famous songwriter and producer called Tony Hiller. Tony has been very successful in the music business and wrote such hits as 'United We Stand' and 'Save All Your Kisses For Me', but back then they were all just young Cockney boys trying to make a living in show business. Terry was very optimistic about the possibilities, but I don't believe any of the songs were published. Every week he'd get the same reply: 'No thanks, but keep trying.'

He met some very interesting people during his time up there. Terry's agent these days is a man named Eric Hall, and the first time he met Terry was in Tin Pan Alley. Eric was an office boy for one of the companies and nephew of Tony Hiller, and he and Terry became great friends. They shared a love for music and great singers including Sinatra, Tony Bennett, Sarah Vaughan and Billy Eckstine, and when they start talking about songs and songwriters they're in another world. Eric went on to become a plugger for a record company, and has always made a living out of the record business. Now he works as an agent for a number of famous actors, actresses and many footballers, including Terry.

Another Denmark Street office boy at the time was Elton John, then working under his real name, Reg Dwight. Elton was making the tea back then, and Terry and a lot of the other lads would send him out for sandwiches or a packet of fags. It's astonishing to think of him then and see how successful he is now, but the old saying is true – everyone has to start somewhere. Terry still liked the company of the Tin Pan Alley people even when he went to Spurs, and he'd make regular trips up there with his pals at Tottenham, Phil Beale and Joe Kinnear.

Another musical mate of Terry's was the jazz band leader, Kenny Ball. Kenny was Dagenham born and bred from Walnut Tree Road, but ironically the first time the pair met up was on the other side of the world in Australia. As young boys in Dagenham, they were the local celebrities and every time Terry went into the fish and chip shop, the owner, Mr Weston would tell him. 'Kenny Ball's just been in here, you've missed him by minutes.' They would leave messages for one another to meet up for a drink, but never quite got round to it. Then, by coincidence, Terry was on tour down under with Chelsea, while Kenny was over there with his Jazzmen. I don't know how, but a local television company discovered the Dagenham connection and got Terry to an airport to meet Kenny off a plane. What a surprise after all those near misses in the local chippy, and Terry and Kenny's smiling faces made big news in many of the Australian papers.

Terry did finally realize one musical ambition – in Spain, when he sung live with a big band on one of their top television shows. It was shortly after he had won the Championship with Barcelona, and the producer had heard that Terry was once a nightclub singer. He invited him on for an interview, then gave him the opportunity to sing Sinatra's 'I've Got You Under My Skin'. The band played the arrangement written for Sinatra by Count Basie, and Terry's impression of Old Blue Eyes himself is pretty much spot-on. He looked as if he was having a whale of a time, putting his heart and soul into the big finish. I've got the video of his performance, and it brings a smile to my face every time I see it. The audience went wild at the end and I think most of them were surprised he managed to pull it off, but that's Terry. He was going to be on 'This is Your Life' that year as well, but he found out about it at the last minute and the show was scrapped. It's probably just as well, there's no way they could have packed all that into one half-hour programme.

10

I have Myrtle to thank for making Terry the successful businessman he is today. I think her influence in his formative years gave him a level-headedness and respect for money and good sense that can often mean the difference between success and failure for men once their careers end as professional footballers. When Terry was young he was always taught the value of money for the simplest of reasons – we didn't have any! The money I brought in from the docks and Myrtle's from her cafe, would often be barely enough to see us through the week, and Terry was sensible enough as a young boy to realize this.

He would never just take money to go and buy his fish and chips of a night, he'd ask first, and if he wanted a little bit extra, he'd ask before taking that, too. I might have been tempted to spoil Terry rotten as a boy, being the only child, but not Myrtle. She would always take a hard line with him if she thought he was in the wrong, punishing him by preventing him from playing football with the lads over the park and sending him to bed sometimes without any supper. That was an end to it, as far as she was concerned, but I admit I was often in trouble for sneaking his food up the stairs when I thought she wasn't looking. Often she'd confront me and I would deny it, then I'd slip up there when her back was turned, poke my head round the door and quickly pass him his dinner.

I suppose I was lenient in many ways, but I think we did a good job in bringing Terry up the right way. I can remember Myrtle drumming it in to him as a schoolboy: 'You've got to be top at your lessons as well as your football. Whatever you decide to be you've got to aim to be the best.' I would tell him as well: 'There's no point in being mediocre. If you're going to be a footballer, second-best is nowhere. Anyone can be average, anyone can be ordinary.' We always tried to prepare Terry for anything in life, because we knew a career in football could be short, and could end at any time. Footballers in their prime can be struck down by injury, and we wanted to make sure Terry had other avenues and careers he could pursue.

Myrtle's Welsh upbringing meant she was a very straight, down-to-earth person, and when there was money on offer from scouts in Terry's schoolboy days, it was always Myrtle who insisted we had nothing to do with it. When Terry signed for Chelsea it upset me that certain people thought we had been paid for his signature, because anyone who knew Myrtle would tell you she wouldn't be party to any of that sort of business. If I even harmlessly suggested Terry and I took a trip to a club to talk with the manager, she would be down on us like a ton of bricks. 'Oh no you don't,' she'd say, 'you're not going anywhere, you're not agreeing to anything.' I think it was his mum's strictness that rubbed off on Terry, and to this day he has a very clearly-defined sense of right and wrong.

When he bought his first car, an old Ford, he did it the hard way, working two summers as the attendant of Barking baths to supplement his eighteen-pounds-a-week wage at Chelsea. We had some times with that car! Every morning he would leave it parked at Barking station, then catch the tube up to Stamford Bridge for his full day's work as an apprentice. Terry wouldn't get home until the evening, and one night I received a phone call from him, he was agitated: 'I'm at the station, dad,' he said, 'I can't get home ... someone's nicked my car.' We reported it to the police and a couple of days later we received another call to say it had been found at the chest hospital in Forest Gate, minus the wheels. It was a freezing cold night in the middle of winter, but out I went, wrapped up like Scott of the Antarctic with a set of four replacement wheels. It took me ages to get them on, my hands were numb with cold by the time I had finished. I took the keys off Terry, sat in the driver's seat, turned the ignition ... nothing. Tried it again ... not a sausage. Then we looked under the bonnet to discover the little bleeders had taken the battery as well! By that time we were so fed up we decided to go home and return the next day, hopefully with a bit of sunlight on our backs. It was only an old, second-hand model, but it was Terry's first car and mattered one hell of a lot to him. At first, Terry didn't have much luck with cars at all. His next was a brand new green Hillman Imp and he had three accidents in it, in as many months. His mum took a firm line again. 'Get rid of it, Terry,' she said, and he did! He lost quite a bit of money selling that car.

Myrtle's business sense was usually sound, and it was her idea that Terry should form his own limited company at the age of just eighteen. Terry Venables Ltd was the talk of football back then, in many ways an idea years ahead of its time. But I think Myrtle fully understood the lucrative side-lines football could bring, and wanted to protect her son from the sharks who would try to invest his money in all sorts of hare-brained schemes. It meant that Terry was his own boss at a time when many players are wondering what to do with their money, and the idea was his mum's. She had run a business herself for many years and could point out all the pitfalls. I think it encouraged Terry to live at home until he was twenty-three when he married Christine at a church near West Ham baths.

It was a stabilizing influence, although Terry has never been scared to try anything that he feels will help his professional or business life. I can remember him sending more shockwaves around football by taking up a typing course when he was Tottenham's twenty-five-year-old midfield schemer. Terry had his own business buying and selling job lots, and he thought touch typing would add speed to his business correspondence. He was pictured in one of the newspapers learning to type with a group of secretaries at a school in Oxford Street, and everyone thought it was very strange. But Terry has never been concerned with other people's opinions if he thinks a job is right for him. His attitude was: I've finished training by one o'clock, why not learn to type? It's got to come in useful. It did, in both his business life and his career as a writer with Gordon Williams. When Terry first went into management at Crystal Palace, he recommended to many of the players there that they take up a trade to prepare them for life outside football. He allocated a player to each one of Palace's vice-presidents, who then took the lad around showing him how he did his particular job, or ran his particular business. Unfortunately, one by one, the players all dropped out and the scheme ended. You can lead a horse to water but you can't make him drink, I suppose. It's a shame because many footballers could be a lot more successful in business when their playing careers ended if they only gave it more thought. Certainly, Terry felt in no way embarrassed to be the only boy in a class full of girls, and when he got on to the field with Tottenham, he forgot about the typing altogether and became a player again.

I don't think Terry has ever let his interests outside the game conflict with his career as a player and manager. Often he's been able to turn his business brain to some good. Geoff Bradley, a business partner of Terry's, had a five-year-old son Ricky whose eyesight was saved by doctors at the Institute of Ophthalmology in London. Terry would often go in to see him, but one day a doctor told him they had problems with the research unit through underfunding. That was when Terry and Geoff came up with the idea of the Fight for Sight appeal.

They noticed a lot of people threw old newspapers out at the end of the day, and realized that paper warehouses could obviously use them for recycling. So they started a campaign collecting old newspapers, and when they had a full van load they would sell it to the warehouses and the cheque would go directly to the institute. Of course, once Terry had started it we all had to join in and I spent virtually all day driving round in a big old Albion van collecting newspapers for charity. Geoff Bradley gave up his job working with Terry to concentrate on the charity and they opened offices in Judd Street, London.

Terry's grandparents, Millie and Ossie, also got involved. They didn't have a car so they would go door-to-door with a pram, filled to the brim with papers – it was quite a picture. We had the local boy scouts group helping us, and at the end of the day everything would be unloaded and piled into Terry's garage. We had tons of the stuff, so much that I had to give up driving the van and employ a full-time driver, because there was no time left for me to go to work.

This carried on for months and months, with the scouts

loading the vans up and my driver shipping it out to the warehouses. Terry lent his name to the campaign, and was very involved, collecting papers in his area. It was a brilliant idea, because people were only going to sling the old newspapers in a dustbin anyway. Terry said from the start: 'Don't ask them for money, ask them for paper.' Terry and Geoff's idea finally raised £100,000 for charity.

Over the years I have expanded my own business interests with Terry, and the Royal Oak in Chingford is now just one of six pubs under our control. The company we run together is called Transatlantic Inns and we've got pubs in Epping, Marlow and Reading. Things have moved on a lot since the days in Bonham Road and we still have a good father–son relationship. I'll try to guide or advise him if I think he needs it, but there is another side to it now. There'll be an argument from time to time, and we've been known to put the phone down on each other, but we've never let it get to the stage where there has been a blazing row and we've not been able to speak.

Terry has great involvement in everything we do, even though the running of the pubs is meant to be down to me. He will still go round and check out the new sites and every day, no matter where he is in the world, he rings up to make sure everything is all right and ask how trade has been. He checks up on me all the time, asking if I've been up the road to Epping to see if everything is running smoothly. I've never known anyone so quick to come to a decision if something needs to be discussed. It's almost as if the roles have changed over the years, and whereas once me and his mum would look out for him, in later life he has done the same for us.

Terry has always made sure I am treated well at every football club where he has been in charge, and even though his mum moved to Wales until her death this year, he kept in touch regularly by phone and often popped down to see her. In many ways, over the years, we've almost become like brothers. I'm not 'dad' any more, I'm 'Fred', or 'Fred the Ted' if he's feeling cheeky. Once we used to meet regularly at the Royal Oak for a drink and Sunday lunch when Terry lived in Loughton. Now he has his house in Kensington and I'll meet him for a drink at a hotel in the West End.

There are some things that never change and it doesn't matter how successful Terry has become I've always tried to offer advice on certain matters. In many ways, I think that's what fathers are for, to be there to give the second opinion, to say to their sons 'are you sure' when they are rattling on about one scheme or another. I've never tried to talk Terry out of anything in life, not even the job at Barcelona, when I could tell it was a difficult decision for him to make. Terry has never been a bighead or the sort of person who won't listen, and I've never felt the need to lay down the law to him on anything.

It seemed strange to me the first time Terry talked of expanding into different areas of business. One minute I was standing on the touchline watching a schoolkid in baggy shorts, or setting up nets for a game in the park; the next he was talking about a tailor's shop he was planning to open, or a business selling sports equipment. I can remember talking to him about his partnership in the tailor's shop, not lecturing him, but passing on some of the common sense that almost thirty extra years on the planet have given me. 'If there are shares,' I told him, 'make sure everyone has the same amount, and get everything signed and agreed in writing. Don't get in over your head, don't take anything on you can't handle.' Terry would listen, and then off he'd go. There comes a time when you've got to let them make their own mistakes, go out in the world and learn for themselves.

I still have my say, and the area where he will usually bow to my knowledge is the pub game. Football is his world, and

I would never tell him how to run his club, and he doesn't tell me how to run a pub. There have been many times when I've put him right over this plan or that plan, and he realizes I won't stand any arguing. I have the say; I interview the managers, I appoint the staff. He's so busy with football and his other interests I doubt if he would have the time, anyway.

Terry's problem is that he has always been a workaholic. Everything is performed at 100 m.p.h. He lives at that speed, works at that speed, and drives at that speed. I don't know how he sleeps. Probably with his brain racing at the same speed. There have been many times when I have worried that he has taken on too much, but he has always assured me he is in control. Terry's schedule frightens the life out of me. He's often got a meeting to go to at breakfast time, but if not he'll still be out of the house at nine o'clock, having read through the papers, and drive across town to Tottenham's training ground at Mill Hill, north London. Sit in a car with him for ten minutes and the phone will never stop ringing except when he's making calls or returning ones from the night before.

After training, if he doesn't go back to the ground or to a reserve game there will be more meetings with people both in and out of football, or interviews with the Press. If he's not at a game in the evening, scouting for players or checking future opponents, there'll be more activity, more meetings, more engagements to go to, and people to see. I don't think Terry could ever be happy just having one thing on his mind, he'd get bored. Management today is increasingly becoming a twenty-four-hour job. Even at home the phone never stops ringing, and he's got to have one of the busiest answering machines of any man in the world. I think British Telecom would go out of business if Terry moved abroad again.

The only day he seems to be able to relax is Sunday, it's

still his one day off. He might have a lie-in, or read through the newspapers, but then he's off and running again, preparing for the next day's training.

He still goes over to Spain regularly to see friends, and he's kept a villa out there which I run in his absence. You hear about people having heart attacks and there are many times I've advised him to ease up, but it goes in one ear and out the other. He'll say to me: 'You're sixty eight and you're still flying about. What do I need to slow down for?' The difference is my life is busy, his is demanding, and I'm sure I couldn't put up with a lot of the aggro that goes with his job. Managing in England is not like Barcelona, and people always think they know more about your job than you do.

We used to be able to have a drink in the Princess Sophia Hotel in Barcelona, surrounded by fans, knowing that we would hardly ever be disturbed. But I had to ban all football talk in our pub a few years ago, because it was becoming impossible to get any peace and quiet. Terry would be standing at the bar with people saying: 'If you'd hit that cross to the far post just after half-time, there was a man unmarked waiting to score.' It might not seem much, but how would you like people coming up and telling you how to do your job every time you stepped out the door? Not that Terry ever complained, but I began to feel awkward and protective for him, and could see that sooner or later I would have an argument on his behalf.

The places Terry takes me to now, I know I *have to* behave. Often, we'll meet at a posh hotel in central London, and I always make sure to go booted and suited, even if Terry is just moping about in a jumper and casual trousers, and I never carry on as I would if we were in a pub together. I have no regrets about the way his life has changed, even though it means we don't get to spend our Sundays together. When Terry went into football I hoped I would see him at Wembley and Old Trafford, I didn't give as much thought to the commercial side; it was always his mum who took an interest in that. Now I know he has something to fall back on if the football ended tomorrow and that pleases me. Being your own man and financially secure gives you freedom in a lot of ways.

People say the secret of Jack Charlton's success is that he no longer needs football and that's probably true in Terry's case as well. It means if he doesn't like something that is going on he doesn't have to stand for it, he can be his own man and it takes the pressure off. Don't get me wrong, I can hardly imagine a time when Terry will not be involved in football in some capacity, and neither can he. It has been his life since he was old enough to kick a ball, and I'm sure he's lost more sleep and had more fun out of football than almost anything else in his life – it is his passion. I'm also glad Terry has been a success in other fields, whether it is book-writing or business. Everything has been approached with the same positive attitude and he has proved himself a winner.

One of the greatest thrills of my life came when I heard Barking and Dagenham Borough Council were naming a street in the area after Terry – Venables Close in Dagenham. Few people can make a claim to something like that and to see my son's name, my name, recognized like that gave me a thrill I cannot express. You hope for a lot of things in life, but to see people show respect for you as a person in that way makes me so proud. People talk of having five minutes of fame, but Venables Close will be there after I, and probably Terry, have gone and that gives me a special sort of buzz.

I can remember the first time I played a game called Trivial Pursuit. I got the same sort of feeling from discovering that Terry was the answer to two of the questions. I was on a holiday cruise and there were four or five of us playing, and the first question read: 'Which English manager led Barcelona to the Spanish Championship in his first season?' Everyone laughed when it was read out, knowing Terry was the answer. The second was more difficult: 'Who is the only player to have represented England at all six levels – schoolboy, youth, under-21, under-23, amateur and full international?' It wasn't my turn and the first guess was Bobby Moore. Wrong. Bobby Charlton? Wrong again. 'I know,' I said, 'it's Terry.' Correct again. They might seem little things now, trivial as the game's name suggests, but to a lorry driver and former docker from a council house in Dagenham they mean one hell of a lot.

11

It came as no great surprise to me when Terry announced, shortly after his return from Barcelona, that he was to join Tottenham as their manager in November 1987. Firstly, Irving Scholar had been a regular visitor to Spain over the past number of years and I always had a secret thought that one day he would want Terry to manage the club. Secondly, I have found that what Terry sets out to do in life he usually achieves, and his mum still has the schoolbook in which it is written: 'I want to play for Tottenham and manage Tottenham.' I have always believed that Terry could have been a one-club man as a player, had Docherty not arrived at Stamford Bridge, and Chelsea will always hold a special place in his affections.

Yet Tottenham are probably his first love, the club he supported as a boy, and the footballers in the pictures he hung on his bedroom wall back then were invariably wearing the famous white shirts and cockerel crest. Terry saw his first League football match at White Hart Lane, encouraged by the fervour of his schoolmaster George Jackson, and later he would be awarded a special pass which allowed him to sit near the touchline, as a schoolboy Spurs were interested in signing. Terry was so near the game he felt he could almost join in himself, and he used to come back to our house in the evening thrilled at being so close to his heroes. Dave Mackay was always a favourite, and goalkeeper Ted Ditchburn – Terry used to come home marvelling at some of the saves he made. Alf Ramsey, a local Dagenham boy, was Tottenham's right-back and Terry remembers to this day a ferocious penalty which he saw Alf smash into the roof of the net in one of his first visits to White Hart Lane. So I suppose it was only natural that when Tottenham asked him to be their manager after the unfortunate parting with previous boss David Pleat, Terry jumped at the chance.

It meant working with Spurs's chairman Irving Scholar, a man Terry had known for a long while. Irving has always shown a keen interest in football on the Continent and would regularly visit Barcelona, often in the company of his manager of the time, Peter Shreeves. A lot of football people would travel to Spain, and I never knew who I was going to bump into next, drinking with Terry in the Princess Sofia Hotel. But Irving was a more regular visitor than most, and probably the seeds of Terry's soon-to-be business relationship with him were sown over a drink in the bar or on the veranda.

Anyone who knows Irving will tell you he likes a chat, particularly if the subject is football. He and Terry would talk for ages, you could hardly get a word in edgeways, and sometimes I would have a walk and sit in another part of the bar just to get away from it all. But you could see that Irving was interested in Terry's experiences as a manager in Spain, and the different ways he handled the challenges at Barcelona.

They seemed to get on very well, and by the time David Pleat had left Tottenham, Terry was also a free agent having parted company with Barcelona. On the day after Pleat left it was almost taken as read that Terry would be Spurs's new manager and, sure enough, that is how it turned out.

I presume a lot of people would think I would be delighted to have Terry back again and working so close to home after all those years spent miles apart in Spain. Not so. In fact, I was apprehensive at first, and had grown used to our separation. Barcelona wasn't as difficult to accept as I had first thought, and I had grown accustomed to making the regular, short, flights out there to see him. Staying at Terry's apartment meant we probably saw as much of each other as ever, and I know he appreciated the role of being solely responsible for team matters, after the slog of being involved at all levels of the club in English management. Tottenham is such a big job for a manager, and I was dubious at how easily he'd settle back into the routines of League management after more than three years abroad. But he was so confident and optimistic that I never doubted for a moment he could do it. Of course, I had been to Tottenham many times since Terry left the club as a player in 1969, but I think it is only when you observe something from close-up that you begin to really know how it works, and there had been a lot of changes made since Bill Nicholson's day.

Tottenham was no longer the club of bone china tea cups, and a board totally distant from the general public. It was a public company now, with shareholders and executive boxes, and a board controlled by younger, go-ahead businessmen. In many ways my first trips to Tottenham with Terry in charge were as awe-inspiring as my early visits to Barcelona. Tottenham was an industry now, the football club only an arm of one big company. I have never seen a club as big and powerful as Barcelona, but Tottenham comes close. One look at the impressive new stand with its many floors housing club offices and function rooms is an indication of how football has changed. I'd never seen anything like it in English football, and on match days the security and officials patrolling the stadium are vast.

I'll never forget Barcelona's militia, with their yard-long truncheons and dogs, but believe me, Tottenham on match days take some beating when it comes to blokes in uniform strolling around with walkie-talkies! In many ways, Barcelona is behind the times. Things haven't changed at Nou Camp in twenty years; directors and presidents have come and gone but the running of the club has never altered. Tottenham, you can see, experienced an explosion when the club became a public company. Suddenly there were new possibilities, new areas to be explored and you can see how the club has grown and grown in such a short space of time.

In many ways the build-up to Terry's arrival at Tottenham was even worse than the build-up he had received in Barcelona. In Spain, he was a nobody, the Press slated him before a ball had been kicked, other managers predicted he wouldn't be able to do the job. In one way, it put him under a lot of pressure in his first matches, but in another he couldn't lose. If no-one expects you to win, you can go out with nothing to lose. 'Everyone thinks I'm a failure anyway, what the hell,' is the attitude. It can also bind a team and manager together into taking the critics' words and stuffing them down their throats. But at Tottenham ...?

Terry was heralded as the second coming – he would have had to walk on water to live up to his billing. He was to be their saviour, the man who would bring the Championship to White Hart Lane for the first time since they won the double in season 1960–61. It was nonsense really. Terry hadn't even arrived at the club and already he was being talked of as the man who would succeed where others, including Terry Neill, Keith Burkinshaw and David Pleat had failed. I couldn't understand it. If the Championship is so easy to win, clubs like Spurs and Manchester United wouldn't go more than twenty years without it, and I could see more was expected of Terry here than at any of his previous clubs.

He had taken on both Crystal Palace and Queens Park Rangers when they were out of the First Division and his target then was to get them promotion. But Tottenham had finished third in their previous season, and for the fans it was the title or bust. Terry admits now he had no idea about the sort of work that needed to be done to turn the club around. Tottenham's high League placing had been achieved with the famous five-man midfield, and Clive Allen on his own upfront scoring almost fifty goals in probably the greatest season of his life. But Glenn Hoddle, the man who made that midfield tick, had left in the summer for French club Monaco in a transfer worth one million pounds. Clive had announced that he would be going, too, once his contract expired at the end of Terry's first season. Defender Richard Gough had recently left for Graeme Souness's Rangers and with players like goalkeeper Ray Clemence, brilliant Argentine midfielder Ossie Ardiles and, most unfortunately, defender Danny Thomas coming to the end of their careers, Spurs wasn't the doddle that people thought. Particularly with every newspaper pundit telling the fans Terry was the new Bill Nicholson!

Terry's first two games didn't go well and Spurs were beaten by Liverpool and Charlton, and there was more embarrassment on the way when they were knocked out of the FA Cup by Third Division Port Vale. It was no great disaster, and the team rallied well enough to finish mid-table, with Terry now well aware of the job on his hands. He made two big signings that summer, and brought Tottenham fans into contact with one of the greatest characters the game has produced – Paul Gascoigne.

A lot of clubs were interested in Gazza, but it was a question of who would have the bottle to sign him. He played football wearing a smile as wide as the Tyne Bridge, and sometimes his sense of fun and the jokes he liked to have with opponents and referees would get him into trouble.

Terry has always liked to have strong characters in his side, and I well remember his comments about football being played in cemeteries unless players tried to put a sense of fun and enjoyment into the game. As both a player and manager a lot of his teams have been associated with giving the supporters something to laugh and talk about, whether it was Rodney Marsh and Stan Bowles at QPR, or Crystal Palace's young and exciting promotion-winners.

Terry had seen a lot of Gazza in his first season back in England. Newcastle were willing to sell and Terry knew Manchester United had also been monitoring the situation. The transfer fee, two million pounds, seems in no way expensive now that Paul is an England regular. Tottenham could probably get four times that if Gazza decided to leave tomorrow. He's a brilliant chap, and a real boost to have in the dressing-room, and there are many funny stories about his antics. Whenever the players come back from international duty with England, there's always at least one new Gazza story to tell.

For instance, two years ago he was picked for an England B tour of Switzerland, Iceland and Norway, with two other Tottenham players Paul Stewart and Gary Mabbutt. The second match of the tour was on a Friday night in Reykjavik, and the freak weather conditions even had the natives complaining. It had been raining all day, and the pitch resembled a paddy field. Then two hours before kick-off a howling wind began to blow from east to west, sending the stinging rain into everyone's faces – and this was in the middle of May! The temperature was sub-zero, and there were some suggestions the game would be postponed. In these conditions, England's manager Dave Sexton sent the players out to 'warm up' in front of the five hundred fans brave enough to venture outside their doors for the night's match. The arrival of the England players on the pitch coincided with that of the brass band, dressed in smart white uniforms with matching white instruments, whose job it was to play the national anthems and entertain the crowd before kick-off. Their leader was a very self-important-looking man who positioned himself on the conductor's stand, tapping his stick several times and demanding quiet, and then poised himself ready to begin the evening's musical overture. This was too much for Gazza to resist and he sent a forty-yard crossfield ball which missed the conductor's head by inches, almost knocking him off the podium. An honest mistake, he decided, and signalled for the band to begin. However, their striding military theme became a cacophony as the band were bombarded with long kicks from Gazza, who had now made his target the bell of a large tuba on the end of the second row. He had the entire England team supplying him with passes as he showered the band in footballs, and the crowd loved every minute of the fun. It was only when Dave Sexton heard the cheers that he realized what was happening, and brought the warm up to a swift end!

Gazza's sense of fun is never-ending, and on his first trip with England's full squad he had all of them in hysterics with his antics over the dinner table. Picture the scene: England's twenty-two man squad, the Football Association's international committee, England's coaches, and manager Bobby Robson are all seated in a plush hotel restaurant waiting to be served, when Gazza, the new-boy in the squad, turned to his manager and asked straight-faced: 'Can I have a word with you, boss?' Robson, thinking Gazza was looking for coaching advice, or perhaps a word about his role in the team, replied: 'Of course, son, do you want to speak here or in private?' 'Here will do fine.' By now, there was a hushed silence around the table. 'What's on your mind, son,' asked an unsuspecting Robson. 'I was only thinking,' said Gazza, 'that you're looking ever so old, man. Your hair's all grey and your face is full of wrinkles – what's going on?' Poor old Bobby didn't know what to say, and everyone broke up into helpless laughter.

Gazza doesn't just hand out stick, he can take it, too. When he first came to Tottenham he was probably a stone overweight, caused by his liking for Mars bars, crisps and junk food of all kinds. Visiting fans are very quick to pick up on that sort of thing, and whenever he stepped on to the field there would be chants of 'fatty'. The joke grew and grew until it became commonplace for Gazza's arrival to be greeted with a hail of mini-size Mars bars from the opposing terraces. With the joke now on him, Gazza proved he could take it, simply picking up the Mars bars and stuffing them down his socks, as if saving them for an after-match treat, or pretending to eat them there and then. Once, when the jokes about his weight were at their height, he even stuffed the ball up his shirt and kidded the fans he had a gut the size of Bernard Manning's!

He's certainly brilliant fun to have around, and I'm sure he's almost as invaluable for the spirit he gives the team off the field as for his performances on it. He's the sort of bloke who will have the lads crying with laughter as he picks out chopsticks on a piano, or pretends to play like Les Dawson, and he's just as capable of pulling the same gag at the Savoy Hotel in the middle of afternoon tea.

Only last season he pulled an incredible stunt, just as the team bus was about to leave for an important away match. Tottenham train at a ground in Mill Hill, just off the junction of the M1 and A1, and there are always groundsmen and friends of the club about to prepare the pitches and help keep the place tidy. One day, one of these blokes, a pal of Nayim's, was loading some empty boxes on to the top of one of the club vans, when Gazza walked past. 'What are you doing that for?' he asked. 'We're going to need them.' So Nayim's mate climbed a ladder attached to the van's back doors and began to unload the empty boxes. No sooner was he up the top when Gazza seized his chance. Up he jumped into the cab and drove the van off across the car park at break-neck speed, with the poor bloke clinging on to the back for dear life. All anyone could hear was a blood-curdling scream as Gazza threw the van this way and that, with the bloke hanging from the back like a kite. This went on for a good five minutes, with Gazza taking the van out in to the street for a couple of wheel-spins before eventually coming to a halt allowing the white-faced helper to stagger to the ground.

That's typical of Gazza, he's like the naughtiest boy in the class and Terry often describes him to me as mischievous. He's not a nasty lad or a bad boy, more the sort who used to walk behind the teacher pulling faces, then went red as a beetroot when he was caught! I feel sorry for him at times, because his behaviour doesn't go down so well with every-body, and he is often criticized for not taking the game seriously enough. It was Bobby Robson who called him 'daft as a brush' and the next week Gazza played along with the gag by going out on to the pitch with a tiny hairbrush stuck down the front of his sock. Deep down, I think some of the criticism hurts him, and I truly hope he goes on to prove many of his critics wrong. I know Terry feels he will become an even greater player for his country, and I agree.

Of course, Terry was especially delighted at Gazza's per-formance in the 1990 World Cup. It's always nice to have your decisions vindicated, and everything Terry had been saying about the lad in the last two seasons has been proved correct. He stuck on Gazza's side when everything was going against him, when people, including the England manager Bobby Robson, had their doubts. Right from his very first days at Tottenham, Terry maintained Gazza would one day be an outstanding international player. Yet even then he was knocked for buying him. Only Manchester United were interested, and big clubs like Liverpool, Arsenal and Everton all had a look but didn't want to know. The fee of two million pounds was thought too big, and a lot of people regarded Gazza as just a young lad with a few jokes, who was overweight and didn't take his football seriously enough. But Terry knew different. He had seen another side of Gazza, a sensitive side, a boy who thought about his football and cared deeply for his family. Sure enough, Gazza will play up from time to time, and not everyone finds his stunts amusing. But if he thinks he has hurt someone he will always run back and make sure everything is alright. Terry liked what he saw in him and they got on from the first day they met. He admired Gazza's confidence and cockiness – something common to all great players – and also the way he thought carefully about his future and his decisions. All teams need big characters like Gazza, and Terry could see his off-field presence becoming every bit as valuable as his performances on it.

That is why he showed faith in Gazza right the way through from his first game for Spurs to his eventual call-up into the England squad. He told him off from time to time, when he needed it, but Gazza is naughty, not bad, and is not as much of a handful as people think. And whatever criticisms can be made of Terry, it can never be said that he didn't spot Gazza's genius from the start. He always felt he would make an England star, and that hunch became a certainty after watching him in action in a friendly against Czechoslovakia. At that time there was still a question mark over whether he would go to the World Cup, and Robson had given him this match to prove himself once and for all. Gazza felt there was so much pressure on him, he even came to talk it over with Terry in the week before the match. Terry gave him it straight – you can either use the pressure as an excuse and have a bad game, or go out and show everyone what a great player you are, putting all the pressure on your critics. Terry said he knew within minutes of the kick-off what course Gazza had chosen. He was brilliant in England's four-goal victory, and after that everyone knew he was going to stay the course all the way to Italia 90.

England's first World Cup game against the Republic of Ireland was difficult, but against Holland with the new sweeper system, Gazza really stood out. It was pleasing for Terry because he had long maintained that playing five men in defence would be the way to get the best out of Gazza. And, sure enough, as the tournament went on Gazza got better and better. Terry made regular appearances in the BBC studios as an expert, and he was often asked about his man. It must have been a real temptation to say to the world: 'I told you so!', but Terry is not one to gloat. Anyway, Terry's views had been so publicly aired and said with such conviction, there can hardly have been a man alive who didn't already know he had been telling them so! I know Terry really felt for Gazza the day his and England's World Cup came to an end against West Germany in the semi-finals.

Franz Beckenbauer's side beat England on penalties after extra time, and went on to win the World Cup. That was bad enough, particularly as England gave as good as they got – if not better. But worst of all was Gazza's booking, his second of the tournament, which would have put him out of the Final had England got there. The sight of Gazza crying with disappointment on Robson's shoulder was too much for me, and a lot of people. I know people who cried with him – I know others who didn't even want England to get to the

Final if Gazza was not to be involved. That is the hold this man now has over the public, it's almost as if he can do no wrong. And he's proved himself a sensible lad, getting his Gazza nickname made into a trademark on his return, so it can only be used with his permission. That move took a lot of people by surprise, but I see it as shades of Terry becoming Terry Venables Ltd at the age of seventeen – ahead of its time. Now an England team without Gazza is unthinkable, as Terry predicted it would be. Everywhere he goes Terry is asked if Gazza is going to one of the world's rich clubs in Spain or Italy. But he is adamant he will not be sold – not even for ten million pounds. What is the point of bringing a lad through and then letting him go when he is nearing his peak? And, believe me, Gazza's best is yet to come.

Terry's other signing that summer was Paul Stewart from Manchester City for one and a half million pounds, and Terry has taken a lot of criticism since over that transfer. I've always thought a manager can only act on the information he has been given, and the scouts' report on Paul that season had been uniformly excellent. Having only just returned from Barcelona, it was impossible for Terry to know the ins and outs of every footballer in the League, and his scouts were kept busy all season checking on new talent. Their verdicts on Paul were so strong that Terry had several looks himself, and every time he played impressively. I went with Terry to watch one game, and I agreed that Paul looked quick, strong and aggressive, just what Tottenham needed upfront with Paul Walsh. Any talk of Terry plunging into the transfer market in a panic is just rubbish. Once he had made up his own mind, he took Irving Scholar to watch several of Paul's games, and together they came to the conclusion that he was the man.

Terry's transfer dealings at Tottenham will always come under close scrutiny because of the amounts involved. Managers at smaller clubs, dealing in one hundred thousand pound players, are very rarely held up for question, but Spurs have to be seen to be spot-on all the time. No-one could have envisaged the problems Paul has had in settling down south, but if he does, I am sure he will show he is worth the money. No-one becomes a bad player overnight, and there have been many times when Paul has shown what he can do.

Chris Waddle was outstanding for Terry in his second season at Tottenham, and it was a very controversial decision to sell him to Marseilles for four-and-a-half million pounds in summer 1989. But I could understand Terry's reasoning – Waddle was twenty-nine, and once he had heard of Marseille's interest and the money involved, the decision to leave had to be left to Chris. Terry tells of the negotiations with Marseilles and of rejecting bids of three and four million. Even when the bidding went higher they would still have turned it down, but there was now a duty to tell Chris. Had he found out at a later date, he would probably never have forgiven Terry for blocking his opportunity to be set up financially for life.

The money from Waddle's transfer gave Terry the opportunity to bring Gary Lineker back from Barcelona, and that is a move that has paid off in fine style. It says a lot for Terry as a manager that Gary wanted to work with him again, and his goals last season pushed Spurs above the former League Champions and north London rivals Arsenal in the League.

The one thing that has upset me about Terry's time at Tottenham is the criticism he has received in the Press for spending money on players. I get sick of picking up the papers to read people like Emlyn Hughes, Tommy Smith and Docherty, having a go at Terry over his transfer market dealings, and I know it frustrates him to be continually forced to put the record straight. With the money from Chris Waddle and other sales at Tottenham, including Clive Allen and Steve Hodge, Terry is little more than one million pounds down in the transfer market, and certainly not the seven or eight million his critics claim.

I think once you get to a certain level in football, or in life, people are always willing to have a go at you. Terry has been accused of refusing to shake hands with managers after matches, which is another ridiculous claim. Often he has been dashing to dressing-rooms and has been too busy as the game ends, but he'll always have a drink and a chat with opposition managers once the hullabaloo has died down, and many of them have been his friends for years. His 'feud' with Brian Clough is a case in point, because I know the two spoke on the phone quite amicably to each other shortly before the end of last season.

Terry was at a reunion lunch with a lot of his ex-Chelsea team-mates when a waiter came over to tell Terry there was a phone call for him. To his astonishment, he heard the unmistakable tones of Cloughie at the other end and they talked for quite some while. 'We've kissed and made up,' he joked with me. 'Brian brought the kiss and I supplied the make-up!'

Terry has never been a man to seek out controversy. Even in his dealings with players he has always made sure they get a fair hearing and he is not what you would call a disciplinarian as a manager. Of course, there are times when every player has to be put in his place – I'm sure Terry did, too – but he is not one to read the riot act unnecessarily. He learned a lot from his time with Malcolm Allison at Crystal Palace, and watching his coaching even now you can still see Malcolm's influence. I think that is the sector of management he enjoys most: dividing the players into groups, and getting them to do different things so that the sessions never become monotonous. There's not much about management that

Terry does not know after almost fifteen years, and hopefully it will pay off at Tottenham.

12

I've had some great times and met some great people through my involvement with Terry and with football, and I've already told you about many of them. Many of my favourite memories come from when Terry was a kid, just starting out in the game, and I'll never forget the first time I met Allan Harris. Allan was to go on to become Terry's assistant at Crystal Palace, Queens Park Rangers, Barcelona, and in his first two seasons at Tottenham, but I was first introduced to him as a fifteen-year-old apprentice, like Terry, on Ted Drake's staff at Chelsea.

It was Guy Fawkes night, 1958, when Allan came to our house in Bonham Road for a party. He and Terry were very close, and Terry kidded him to put a banger through the letter box of a lady who lived opposite, named Ada. He sneaked across, lit the blue touchpaper, shoved it through and ran. By now Terry was on the other side of the road, and he disappeared laughing into our house, closing the front door behind him. Suddenly, Ada's door opened and out she came, through a cloud of smoke, coughing and spluttering and obviously not in the least bit amused. She was looking for the culprit and Allan, now standing in the middle of the road between the two houses, stuck out like a sore thumb. With that Ada picked up a broom handle and chased him up the street, walloping him all the time, like a scene from Tom and Jerry. He was known as 'Sticky' for years after that, but few people could ever work out why. Good old Ada is still going strong and still lives in the area. There was an article in our paper, *The Dagenham Post*, a short while ago, describing the memories the people of Bonham Road had of Terry. Ada didn't mention the firework, but she did say he used to eat all the jam tarts when the kids came to her house after playing football in the park. All the other boys made a dive for the sandwiches, but Terry has a sweet tooth like mine, and always went for the cakes. The Knave of Hearts she used to call him.

Another close friend of Terry's in his Chelsea days was Ronnie Handley. When Chelsea took Terry on as a professional at seventeen, Ron was kicked out and Terry suggested I get him a job in the docks. I didn't like to say no, but Ronnie was such a harem-scarem type I felt sure he would let us all down. As he was Terry's mate I got him work, and gave him a stiff talking-to before he started. 'I know what you're like, Ron,' I said, 'and I'm telling you now you've got to stay in this job at least a month or I'll be for it.' 'Yes, Mr Venables,' he said. I must have made an impression because he's still there today!

Terry's mates were a funny lot, all just starting out in the game. They were very keen and anxious to impress and they'd do anything if they thought it would help them. A chap named Peter, who Terry played football with on Saturday mornings, was on his way to a match and stopped at a café in Aldgate to have a strawberry milkshake. Peter's team won that day and from then on he'd drive to Aldgate every Saturday to have the same drink. Terry had his own superstitions, spinning the ball on his finger as he ran out, then kicking it into the net.

The greatest match preparation of them all involved Jimmy Greaves in his days at Chelsea. Jimmy was living in Hornchurch, Essex, by then and when Terry made the first team at Chelsea, he would generously offer him a lift in on match days in his pale blue Ford Popular. Terry was only sixteen-and-a-half and still very anxious to be seen doing everything right. On their way in to a game against West Bromwich Albion, Jimmy pulled the car over outside a restaurant near the roundabout at Gants Hill. 'Fancy a bit of lunch?' he asked Terry, 'I always stop here.' Terry was delighted and five minutes later they were seated at a table with Jim greedily surveying the menu. 'What do you fancy?' he asked Terry. 'Boiled chicken on its own, I think,' said Terry, mindful of the match ahead. Jimmy nodded sagely. 'Good choice,' he said, 'right – I'll have roast beef, Yorkshire pudding, some boiled, some roast and a couple of veg. That should do it.' He then went out and scored four as Chelsea beat West Brom 5–0 – so football's dieticians have been doing it wrong all these years!

A few years later, Terry found himself captain of Chelsea, introducing his team-mates to the Duke of Edinburgh before an important match. 'This is Joe Fascione,' he said, 'who is playing his first game.' 'You mean he has never played football before?' asked an incredulous Duke. 'I've never known to this day whether or not it was a joke,' Terry told me.

Chelsea was also the club for celebrity supporters and through his other connections with the West End, Terry became very friendly with song-and-dance man Tommy Steele. One night the boys all went out up town in Terry's old Ford Consul, which had a stick-on aerial, and everyone was coming up to Tommy and asking for his autograph. He was at the height of his fame and very well-known for his television and film work. For a joke, Tommy picked up the aerial and began to interview people, pretending it was a radio microphone. The idea caught on, and very soon the car was surrounded by people all under the impression they were being interviewed live on radio by the famous Tommy Steele. It was like Candid Camera, and the other chaps in the car were falling about laughing.

Sometimes I would go up the West End to meet Terry, but I always tried to keep myself to myself. I had an old van, with no tax and insurance and steam coming out of the engine, and I'd hide it away from prying eyes. After Chelsea won the first leg of the League Cup Final, there was a big party in one of the top hotels and Clement Freud was among the guests. Every time we had another beer, Terry would put a short in it, until we were all completely legless – Clement Freud particularly. 'Show me how you scored that last goal, Terry,' he kept saying, and by that time Terry was ready to oblige. He grabbed hold of a ball and plonked it on the floor. 'I got it like this,' he was saying, 'and then I . . .' and he gave the ball such an almighty crack it flew clear across the room and through a window! We all got into trouble for that.

It has never failed to amaze me how star-struck people can become in the presence of footballers. I've been in the company of big stars like Michael Caine and felt a bit awe-struck, but I'll never forget the day Shirley Bassey asked Terry for his autograph. We were going into Langan's Restaurant in Mayfair as she was coming out, and stood talking for a while. I've been a fan of hers for a long while, but when I asked for her autograph she said: 'Certainly, so long as I can have your son's for my little boy.' It seemed strange to me – a big star like that, asking for Terry's signature.

But back to football, and one of the greatest story-tellers I have ever met was Terry's first manager at Chelsea, Ted Drake. Ted went back a long way and used to tell of the time he scored four goals in a game for Arsenal and met the club chairman, an old boy, in the corridor near the dressing-rooms after the game. Seeing the Arsenal crest on his blazer, the chairman quickly realized he was in the company of one of his players, but was at a loss to know quite who. 'And who are you?' he said, aristocratically. 'I'm Ted Drake,' came the reply. 'I just scored four goals.' 'Oh, jolly good,' said the chairman, and walked off.

Another famous football story concerns Ted as a dashing young striker in his days at Arsenal, although it has since been attributed to many others. At the time, players were paid less during the summer months than they were in the winter and Ted had to see his manager to sort out his wage packet. There were a queue of players waiting to go in, and the player before Ted left the manager's office enthusing: 'Great – I've got eight pounds in the winter, six in the summer.' But when Ted went in, the going rate had dropped. 'I'll give you eight and five,' said the boss. 'But you gave Joe eight and six,' said Ted. 'But he's a better player than you,' insisted the boss. 'Not in the summer he's not,' Ted then replied.

His other joke was to tell players he dreamt they were at Wembley, receiving the FA Cup from the King. They fell for it every time. 'But there's a Queen on the throne, boss.' 'Yes, son, but by the time you get there we'll have a King back.'

Another of Terry's favourite bosses was Liverpool's Bill Shankly, and I can recall Tommy Smith, Terry's marker in one game, telling him of Shankly's pre-match team-talk before one of our games at Anfield. 'You'll be marking Venables today,' he told Smith, 'and I want you to watch him like a hawk and stick with him wherever he goes, particularly if he starts running quickly into a wide position.' 'Why's that boss?' 'Because it's half-time.'

On another occasion, Shankly sent his long-suffering chief scout Geoff Twentyman on a mission to check out future European Cup opposition, a Russian side. Twentyman dutifully made the horrendous journey, which took days to complete and finally arrived back in Liverpool not long before the match. By the time he had prepared his comprehensive report, containing details of each player's strengths and weaknesses it was the morning of the match. The team were gathered for a lunch-time meeting when Shankly spread the report out before him. 'Now Geoff's been over to have a look at them,' he began, 'and the goalkeeper Androp ... the goalkeeper Andropopo ... the goalkeeper Andro ...' There was a short silence. 'Och, to hell with them,' said Shankly, flinging Twentyman's handiwork over his shoulder, 'who cares about them, anyway!'

On another occasion, Shankly was asked his opinion of Rodney Marsh after he had given a brilliant performance against Liverpool. He spoke of him quite highly, and a reporter asked how Marsh compared to Shankly's great hero, Tom Finney. There was a hushed silence as he replied: 'Looking at it now, I think he's got a slight edge over Tom.' Then, with a twinkle in his eyes, he added: 'Mind you, Finney's sixty-five next week.'

Shankly, along with Sir Matt Busby and Malcolm Allison, was one of the managers Terry most admired, and long before Terry's time he was one hell of a player with Preston North End. There is a legendary story about Shankly's appearance in the 1938 FA Cup Final in which Preston beat Huddersfield with a last-minute penalty, given away by centre-half Alf Young. He had tears in his eyes as the ball went in, only to hear Shankly say in this thick Scottish brogue: 'Aye, and that's not the first one you've given away, either.'

I think a lot of the best players have a cheek and wit to go with their talent – Paul Gascoigne is a typical example – and Terry was no exception in his days at Chelsea. Playing against Italian side Roma at Stamford Bridge, Chelsea were awarded a free kick and Terry made a great play of pacing out the ten yards for the Roma wall to get back. As he marched forward they moved out of the way to let him through, a Chelsea team-mate played the ball over the top and he scored!

That is nothing compared to the cheek of the man who pretended he was Terry in order to rob a public house of its takings. That also happened while he was at Chelsea, and I was most surprised to be knocked up late one Sunday night by a tall, officious-looking man in a smart suit. 'Mr Venables,' he asked, 'could you tell me the whereabouts of your son Terry last Saturday night?' 'He was here,' I told him. 'Are you sure?' he quizzed. 'Did he sleep at your house?' 'Yes,' I replied, 'anyway, who wants to know?' 'The police,' he added. I almost fell off my chair as he explained Terry was wanted for questioning in connection with a robbery at a pub in Essex. The circumstances were that a man had gone into a pub late on Saturday night; he was wearing a dark blue blazer and tie and claimed he was Terry Venables of Chelsea and England, and that his car had broken down and he needed assistance. He made a big show of waiting and waiting for a supposed friend to arrive, until finally the landlord took pity on him and offered him a room for the night free of charge. Of course, when the landlord woke up the next morning, 'Terry Venables' had disappeared – along with the previous night's takings! The police were ready to take the landlord's story at face value, until we managed to prove that the real Terry Venables had spent the night with his girlfriend Christine, before returning to sleep in his bedroom in Bonham Road.

I suppose that's one of the drawbacks of being in the public eye, and Terry's had more than his fair share of scrapes. When he was manager of Crystal Palace he was sitting on the bench watching a match, when suddenly there was a terrible commotion in the stand behind. Voices were getting louder and louder and a punch-up started. The police waded in and pulled out one man still shouting and swearing and resisting arrest. Finally, they got him under control and, with his arm up his back, he was dragged from the stand and paraded around the perimeter of the ground before being slung outside. As he came past the bench it was obvious he'd taken the worst of the beating and he had a big, red, bruise, like a tomato, around one eye. To everyone's astonishment, shortly before being taken down the tunnel, he shouted over his shoulder: 'The things I do for you, Tel!'

One of the greatest honours of Terry's life was the day he was asked to manage the Rest of the World team against England, as part of the Football League's centenary celebrations, but what a fiasco that turned out to be. Terry's squad included such great names as Diego Maradona and Michel Platini, but when Terry arrived at Wembley he discovered a dressing-room completely bereft of any of the basic essentials: first aid kit, bucket, sponge and so on. It was a complete shambles, and he had to put his hand in his pocket to pull out the eighty pounds to buy the necessary supplies. At the end of the match, he was given a frosty reception by League officials when he asked to be reimbursed. 'OK,' said Terry, 'but there's a Press conference in ten minutes, I'll see what the papers make of it.' The eighty pounds soon arrived.

I've had some marvellous times with Terry over the last forty or so years, and I'm sure there are many more ahead. When I think back to my beginnings in a Dagenham council house, then look around me now, I realize how much his success has changed my own life. I've been to some magnificent places, met some smashing people, and there's very little of it I would change if I had my life over again. The one party I do regret missing was when Terry was at Barcelona. We were invited to a reunion of the Venables clan from all over the world, to be held at the village of Venables, in Normandy.

The name Venables, it is said, is to be found in the Domesday book and can be traced back to the times of William the Conqueror. Looking at Terry now, I'm not in the least bit surprised.

13

by Terry Venables

Now it's time for me, Terry, to do some of the talking. You already know quite a lot about me from my dad, everything from my first pair of tiny football boots to my last season at Tottenham, and my thoughts of Paul Gascoigne and the summer's World Cup. In this, the last chapter, I'd like to talk just a bit about my mum and dad and the effect their influence has had on my life, and then give you some insights into my plans for the future at Tottenham, and some of the hopes and dreams I've still to realize.

I'm an only child and, like most people in that position, can claim to have an especially close relationship with my parents. My dad's influence on me came from his personality and sense of humour which, even though he's now in his late sixties, shows no signs of waning. We still meet at least once a week and speak on the phone every day, and he's always been the sort of man who can brighten your day with a joke or a story. He says that I'm the music buff in the family, but he's got no mean voice himself, and he's like an encyclopedia for his knowledge of the old standards and show tunes. Throw a title at him and he invariably comes straight back with the verse and chorus, and there's few I know who can beat him, or get him to admit he's never heard of a particular tune. My dad's outlook on life meant I never took myself too seriously, only the work I was pursuing at the time, and I believe that attitude has helped me through some of the tougher times in football.

But it was my mum who, I must admit, played the greatest part in directing me the right way and keeping my feet on the ground almost from the day I set foot inside a soccer stadium. More than anything, it was her business acumen that gave me a really solid point-of-view on what I should do with my life and where I should be going. It is hard for me to talk about her now, because she died from lung cancer at two o'clock in the morning of Tuesday, 7 August 1990, while this book was still being written. I feel no book about me would be complete without a proper mention of just how much my mum's attitudes and beliefs shaped the person I am today. Certainly, it was mum's idea that I should explore the business possibilities of a career in professional football, as well as the playing side, and I think my interest in business and financial matters stems directly from her own strengths as a businesswoman – albeit on a smaller scale than the likes of Barcelona and Tottenham. You've heard how she ran a café in Dagenham, and then in later life a pub in Wales, but I don't think it has been explained just how great the latter achievement was. When my mum and dad separated fourteen years ago she returned to Wales, as had always been her intention, and took a pub in the south, right in the centre of the mining belt. She had always dreamed of running her own place back in that area, but it was still a bit worrying to think of her trying to manage all by herself. The pub's regular customers were mostly retired miners and their sons, big strapping hard men, who had set ideas on what they wanted out of their 'local'. But my mum was having none of it, and determined to run her pub her way. She threw out the darts and a lot of the spit and sawdust trappings and set about smartening it all up. The regulars griped and groaned and one by one stopped going, until it looked as if it could be a real struggle. But my mum was a strong-willed lady and stuck to her guns, and slowly the miners and their sons came back to their new-look local. And this time mum made sure the women were allowed in as well – because, astonishingly, they are still not welcome in certain pubs in the south – and single-handedly she managed to change it all around. That's the sort of woman my mum was, and I think I got a lot of the strength and determination in my character from her. She was always a bit of a go-getter. A short while ago, I was lucky enough to have a company ask if they could make a video about me – they were releasing a series of them on people in football – and mum was one of the people they interviewed. In fact, she's the last voice heard, saying how proud she is of me, and I am so delighted that it has turned out like that. After what happened in the summer it's a lasting memory of her, although I still cannot bring myself to watch it at the moment. She even tried to write a chapter for this book, and made a few notes, but in the end she was too ill to complete it. Anyone who has never experienced the death of a parent might not be able to understand this, but there were times when I truly thought I would not be able to cope with it. She had been so active, playing bowls and going to keep fit with her friends even late in life, then going to her club for a few drinks after. We knew she was ill a few months ago, but we weren't told the extent of her illness. She later said she didn't want to worry dad or myself – it seems so silly now. But as soon as we knew she was seriously ill, myself and dad got straight down to Wales to keep her company. A lot of people might find it strange that dad would be on the scene – after all, they had separated fourteen years ago. But they were always a funny couple – they never stopped loving each other, but just couldn't live together.

Dad would send mum a cheque in Wales from time to time, and she used to joke it was her 'stay away money'! But he would pop down and stay quite often and he was always made more than welcome.

When mum died it hit dad and me like a holocaust. I was meant to be in Norway with Spurs on a pre-season tour but there was no way I could go. I should pay tribute to my backroom staff here, my assistant Doug Livermore, coach Ray Clemence, physio Dave Butler, Ted Buxton and Roy, our kit man, because they were bloody marvellous through-out and without them I don't know what I would have done. I had already spent a couple of weeks just sitting in hospital corridors with my dad, but when it finally happened – at two o'clock in the morning – we both found mum's death very difficult to deal with. It shattered me. I was so proud of my mum, she would come out to Barcelona for a few weeks at a time, and we'd just have ourselves to ourselves – they were such happy times. Not having her anymore hurts, and I know it will go on hurting for a long time. But I think people you love deserve that hurt. They don't demand it and they don't want it, but they've given you a lifetime of love and care, and in a way they should have that hurt out of respect. If you don't hurt maybe there is something wrong, although I know that time, too, is a great healer.

In the week that my mum died, my work, all work, just paled into insignificance. But I think I may even emerge stronger, determined more than ever to succeed and do the right things – for mum. I know she would want me to start work again, and in the weeks after her death I threw myself into the job completely.

But having seen mum's life come to an end has changed the way I look at certain things, and it's made me realize how important it is to make life worthwhile and special, because there are too many people whose own existence is just a waste. I have a number of ambitions left in football, and now I know I must not lose time realizing them.

Among them is to manage at international level – particularly in a World Cup – and after the events surrounding the appointment of a new England manager in the summer, I know I will almost certainly have to look outside my own country in order to do this. Commenting on the short-list for the England job after Bobby Robson's resignation is something I have to be careful about, because I realize I am leaving myself open to accusations of sour grapes. But my feelings were both hurt and amazement that I wasn't included alongside Graham Taylor, Howard Kendall and Joe Royle. It would be easy for me just to shut up, let it ride and say nothing, and I'm sure that's what the Football Association would want and expect me to do. But I've got to speak my mind because I know a lot of people who, like me, find the whole thing a mystery. I've sat down and thought long and hard about this, and it would fascinate me to find out exactly what it is I haven't done right and the real reason I wasn't in that three. It was as if the short-list was a deliberate rebuff by the FA and, if that is not the case, why didn't they produce a short-list of, say, four or six. It was as if they set out to prove a point and say: 'We'll show him – he's not even on our short-list.'

I would never dispute that Graham, Howard and Joe are good managers, and I do believe Graham is the right man for the job, the one with all the correct credentials. There's no reason why he should not do well and I sincerely hope he succeeds and puts England right at the top of the tree. What I would dispute is that there are only three managers in England worthy of inclusion on that short-list. I'd put forward another argument – that there are only three managers at the moment who can do the job and please the FA at the same time.

People have said to me on a number of occasions that I am not an FA type and, for the first time, I am beginning to see what they mean. I now believe that only a certain sort of person gets to manage England and, unfortunately, I'm not their type of guy. I would class myself as thoughtful and serious in my attitude towards football, but with a fairly happy-go-lucky attitude to the rest of my life. I take my job seriously, but I never think I take myself seriously – and that's not good enough for the FA. Look at Bobby Robson, look at Sir Alf Ramsey – these FA people don't want you to look as if you enjoy life, they want you to look as if you're suffering all the time. That's not for me. Poor old Alf, he came from an area three streets away from me, yet you couldn't tell that from the way he spoke. He reminded me of that character in Greek mythology with stones in his mouth, speaking seemed to be agony for him. I still have the accent of the people I grew up with in the streets of Dagenham – good luck to Alf, but I could never change and become another person just to land a job with the FA. The same is true of Robson – at times during his eight years with England he looked tortured. I'm convinced the FA prefer their managers conservative and obliging.

That way is not for me. I'd rather be myself and not get the job, than be someone I'm not just to get it. I have always told my players 'be yourself – develop your own personality', and, as long as they do so professionally and in such a way that conforms to the rules of the game, I truly believe that is the way to get the best out of people. But, having told my players 'be yourself' – how could I act any different. I'll admit that when I first came into football I was embarrassed by my London accent and would try to hide the way I spoke. Now I realize all of that is nonsense – it's what I say, not how I say it, that is important.

I've always hated the sort of sayings we have in this country – for instance 'it's not for the likes of you' – and the way we tend to hold kids back and frustrate them. We don't encourage people to go after the bright lights, and I bet there are hundreds of kids who would have achieved far more were it not for the ambition-crushing attitudes of those around them. We tend to chop people's legs from under them, unless they fit our idea of how people are supposed to behave. I'm sure that's what the FA do when they appoint a new manager. If you don't act a certain way, look a certain way and project a certain image, then – sorry son, but it's not for the likes of you!

Yet picking the right manager is hard enough already, without minimizing the possibilities still further. It shouldn't matter whether you are a smiler, miserable as sin, whether you like a drink, a laugh or a big cigar. Can you do the job? – that's all that should count. One of the strangest questions I have ever been asked was by an ex-player who had just gone into management. 'Terry,' he said, 'what do I have to do to act like a manager?' That's how it gets to some people. You hear managers barking orders – 'Son, pick up that piece of paper!' – because they think that will show everybody who is in charge. You shouldn't have to do that to prove a point. For heaven's sake, you don't have to act like a manager – you are a manager! Yet some people put on a suit and become the boss, take it off at seven o'clock for tea and become themselves again. I know plenty of people in football who are not the people the public perceive, but a lot funnier and a lot more human away from the game. But they learn to put on an act, which I would never do. Sure, I'll work hard all day and it's well known that I can't sit still for two minutes – but when it's time to relax I like a glass of champagne and a laugh with my mates.

But that doesn't mean if I've got the hump with a player I can't turn round and say: 'Hey, you – into my office now!' The only thing I would say is that sometimes the strictest managers can make themselves the weakest. If someone is constantly barking orders, telling people off and playing the disciplinarian, in the end no-one will take any notice of him. I think it's better to leave players uncertain about just how you would react to something, rather than keep warning them how tough you are. In the end, that attitude becomes like a nagging wife – she's always going on, so no-one pays any attention. And, believe me, a manager can shout and holler all he likes – if he's not the right man for the job he's heading for the bullet, no matter how strict he is with the players.

But I've digressed, and I really wanted to tell you about my thoughts on the England job, and any future I may have as an international manager. Put simply, after what happened in the summer I now regard the prospect of managing my country as a thing of the past. But that doesn't mean I might not turn up at a World Cup in a few years time as manager of another country. On the Continent they have a different approach to international management. It's a good job, but not the best job. I discovered that big clubs like Barcelona and Real Madrid often prefer their managers to have international experience before they are appointed – not the other way round as it is in this country. International management is a normal job, and that has set me thinking. There is no reason why I could not manage a country not my own, and if the same people are involved at FA level in a few years time, I am not sure I would even want to manage England if the opportunity arose.

I haven't been terribly impressed by some of the people I have met on behalf of the Football Association, and I find their actions this summer both strange and amusing. Strange, because I would have thought a successful career managing Barcelona in Spain would have counted for something when they were going through the suitable candidates for the England job. I am not being presumptuous when I say I would have expected to be included in any batch of three. Amusing, because the more I look at the sort of people who made the final decision, the less aggrieved I feel that I wasn't asked for an interview. These are people most football fans – and many managers and players, too – would not recognize if they tripped over them in the street. We all talk about the FA, but few know who they really are. And, I'm sorry, but as much as I like Joe Royle as a man and respect him as a manager, I can't take the FA seriously if they put him on the short-list having never managed higher than Division Two, when I'm out of the running.

The only thing that pleases me is that at least the FA didn't kid to me about my chances. I'll never forget Brian Clough getting asked for an interview when everyone knew he had no chance of landing the job. It was almost as if they had sucked him into playing their political game. They'd let him have an interview, as long as he didn't get the job – and I would have hated for that to happen to me. I'd rather stay a non-starter. But the bottom line is that I've been available for the England job without getting a shot at it and now I'm saying to myself that it's possible I'll have to manage at international level elsewhere. I can live with that.

I hope in this way I can put right the myth that I have worked all my life to one aim – managing England. I'm sorry, but it's simply not true, and when I heard Graham Taylor saying in the summer that he had worked at it for twenty years, my immediate thought was: 'You've got more patience than me, mate!' My mistake was that I used to answer questions more honestly than was wise. If I was asked 'would I like to manage England', I would say yes when I suppose a lot of others wouldn't have got involved. For that reason it got around that managing England was my passion – which could not have been farther from the truth. Actually, I never plan more than a year ahead. For instance, when I went to Crystal Palace my hope was that we would win promotion to the Second Division at the end of my first season, it wasn't some grand scheme involving Palace, management abroad and the England job. I have never planned beyond success at my present club, yet to hear some people talk you'd think I had it all mapped out. How many times have you heard that I knew I was going to Barcelona because I started learning Spanish a year before? It's a load of old rubbish. I didn't have an inkling about Barcelona, and I started learning Spanish for three reasons. Firstly, I could see management opportunities opening up in Spain and the rest of Europe – I didn't want to miss out, as Bobby Robson had done, because I didn't know the language. Secondly, I go to Spain for my holidays. Thirdly, I had just returned from the 1982 World Cup and thought how much better it would have been if I had spoken their language. Perfectly plausible, isn't it? Yet even now I still read that Barcelona was a pre-planned stop on the way to achieving my ultimate goal and managing England. I admit, there was a time when I regarded the national job as the best in football, but the events of the last few months have diminished my feelings for it. I'm no longer interested in managing England – sod 'em, forget it, I'll do something else.

It wouldn't bother me in what part of the world I managed, as long as I felt my efforts were worthwhile and were being taken seriously. Even in lesser-known places like Africa there are chances to bring football through in a country where it is only developing – and still have the opportunity to cause a few shocks on the world stage. But, most importantly, I would like to manage in a World Cup. Even when I work for the BBC, covering it and giving my views in the studio, I love the feeling of involvement you get just from being there. The nearest thing I can imagine to it is Barcelona, with the high profile, pressure and the prestige European games. But I do feel that international management is an older man's game, perhaps even older than I am now. As Don Howe once pointed out, matches come around nine or ten times a year, and apart from that you can relax watching your own players or those of future opposition – it is football management at a far more leisurely pace than you will find in the Football League.

That is why I feel my next move could be, not into international management, but perhaps into the boardroom at an English League club. That's right, Terry Venables wants to be a chairman. I'm getting to the time in my life when I want to be my own boss. I want to work for myself, or with someone else, but not for someone else. I can never imagine a time when I am not involved in football, because this game has been my life. But I can imagine a time, later in my life, when I no longer want to be a manager. I came close at Queens Park Rangers when, for a time, I was running the club with a view to an eventual takeover. In that period, not a cheque could be signed without my permission, yet we were a First Division club – albeit a small one – who had qualified for Europe in our first season. I really enjoyed that, getting my teeth into the business side of football, it has always been something that has fascinated me. A football board game I created with my friend and business partner Paul Riviere, called 'The Manager', is based just as heavily on the financial aspects of football, as the playing aspects. And I would also like to think I could be a better chairman than most. For a start, I'm good at football, not developing property or selling pork sausages like some of the other chairmen – I know every job there is to be done at a club. Not that there is anything wrong with property development or pork sausages, but more and more modern-day chairmen seek a degree of involvement in their club for which they are not strictly experienced. I see an increase in chairmen like Aston Villa's Doug Ellis and Ken Bates of Chelsea who fancy themselves as managers. I think they all want to be the boss – and why not, it's their money that's paying for everything. I would probably be the same as a chairman but I wouldn't lie and give someone else the title of 'manager'. I'd do what they do in Spain and have a coach, someone who looks after the team and is off home by one o'clock. I'd do the rest – and I'd tell him so, not kid that he's really the man in charge. I would do the transfers, the buying and selling and all the day to day running – and if the manager fell ill, well at least I do know how to coach, and it wouldn't be the most terrible thing in the world if I took over for a day. I've been on both sides – I'm not saying I would be any different from the Irving Scholars and the Ron Noades's, but I've done the nuts and bolts of running a football club, and they haven't.

I suppose to run my own football club from top to bottom would qualify as my last great ambition in the game. I've got one year left on my contract at Tottenham, and then maybe I'll have to sit down and do some serious thinking.

Index